MERCEDES-SL & SLC

W113 & W107

ISBN: 1 84155 638 6

CONTENTS

Mercedes-Benz 230SL Automatic 2,306 c.c.

Supplement to Road Test No. 1990, 4 September 1964, of the manual gearbox version

IN the recent road test of the impressive Mercedes-Benz 230SL it was explained that another had been tried, fitted with the Daimler-Benz automatic transmission. Full performance testing has now been completed on this car and our initial comment that the transmission was "among the best in our experience" remains more than ever justified.

A central control, much like that of the manual gearbox, is used for the transmission, but it is like the column lever on other automatic Mercedes models in having the six selections: P, R, 0, 4, 3, 2. For fully automatic driving position 4 is used. With full throttle, upward changes occur at 43 m.p.h. (from second to third), and 69 m.p.h. (into top), both speeds corresponding to 5,800 r.p.m. With less throttle, of course, the upward changes are earlier.

More pressure on the accelerator moves the pedal beyond full-throttle, to work the usual kickdown switch, and the extra travel of the pedal is positive. Unless the car is travelling faster than the governed maximum for the lower gear, a change down takes place at once, giving the extra punch for overtaking. In top gear 65 m.p.h. is the upper limit, above which the kickdown switch will not bring in third, and for the other gears 21 (for second) and 14 (first) are the automatic change-down maxima.

Positions 3 and 2 on the selector control may be regarded as gearbox governors, restricting upward changes; if either is selected, the transmission will not go into a higher gear, though it will still change down when required. The upward restriction is absolute, and in 2, for example, the

transmission will not move into third even if the engine is taken to the recommended limit of 6,500 r.p.m. It follows that extra performance is available by holding the indirects until the rev counter indicates this crankshaft speed. This was the technique used for performance testing.

A refinement of position 2 is that it introduces bottom gear for starts from rest (at 3 or 4, the car moves off in second gear unless kickdown is used), and first gear is held much longer. Instead of at 4,000 r.p.m., the point at which the transmission goes from first to second gear on full throttle, the transmission stays in first right up to 27 m.p.h. (5,800 r.p.m.).

PRICES	£	s	d
Two-door Coupé-Convertible	2,975	0	0
Purchase Tax	620	7	1
Total (in G.B.)	3,595	7	1
Extras (including P.T.)			
Automatic transmission	198	3	4
Occasional rear seat	31	8	4
„ „ „ (leather)	42	5	10
Power-assisted steering	93	0	10

All the preset limits for kickdown changes to a lower gear, as mentioned earlier, can be raised by the selector. In 2 and 3, the preset speeds for kickdown are raised to 21 and 37 m.p.h. respectively.

One must emphasize that these "hold" provisions are simply refinements increasing the versatility of a transmission which works extremely well if left to itself, in position 4. The quadrant has nylon edges ensuring smooth action of the lever. A nice balance is struck between the reluctance of some transmissions to change down until the engine is staggering, and the over-eagerness of others. The 3·75-to-1 final drive of the manual model is used, but indirect ratios differ, first being a higher ratio, and second and third being lower. Thus, although the maximum speed in bottom gear is 27 m.p.h. with either transmission, it is achieved at a lower engine speed—5,800 r.p.m. with the automatic, instead of 6,500 r.p.m. All the indirect gears still seem too low, encouraging fussiness.

The neutral (marked 0) position would be useful if it were ever necessary to give the car a tow-start, but a more frequent function is to eliminate the pronounced creep which occurs at traffic halts. Rather than hold the car on the brakes, it is easier in long delays to slip the lever to 0. An overriding safety device prevents engagement of reverse above 10 m.p.h., and incidentally safeguards the parking pawl. Inadvertent selection of either 2 or 0 could also be disastrous, but the shape of the selector slot prevents it by having these two offset, while the 3 and 4 positions are in line with each other.

For fast cornering, overtaking or zooming up hills, the ease with which the lever can be slipped from 4 to 3 is delightful, allowing a smooth change down to third, with full engine braking. The only possible weakness of the setup is that, if the driver uses the lever to select third in readiness for quick overtaking and then treads a little too hard on the accelerator, inadvertently working the kickdown, the transmission may change down to second. After this has happened once, little forethought is needed to prevent a recurrence.

Both the performance and fuel consumption figures need qualification. When we tested the manual gearbox version of the 230SL the hardtop was removed so that the figures

Autocar road test

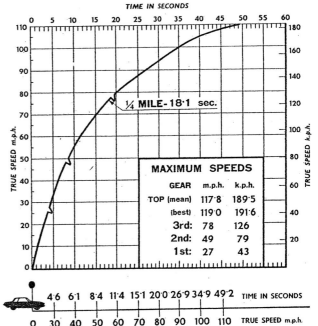

No. 1990a *Supplement to Road Test No. 1990, 4th September, 1964 of the manual gearbox version*

Make · MERCEDES-BENZ
Type · 230SL Automatic
(2,306 c.c.)
(Front engine, rear-wheel drive)

Manufacturers: Daimler-Benz AG, Stuttgart-Untertürkheim, W. Germany

U.K. Concessionaires: Mercedes-Benz (G.B.) Ltd., Great West Road, Brentford, Mdx.

Speed range, overall gear ratios and time in seconds

m.p.h.	Top (3·75) (3·75)		Third (5·93) 5·75		Second (9·45) (8·56)		First (14·9) (16·6)
10—30	—	—		(7·1)	4·4	(4·7)	—
20—40	—	(10·4)	6·5	(6·1)	4·2	(4·0)	—
30—50	11·7	(10·1)	6·8	(6·0)	—	(4·1)	—
40—60	12·1	(10·9)	6·5	(6·1)	—	—	—
50—70	13·2	(10·8)	6·7	(6·3)	—	—	—
60—80	14·3	(12·4)	—	(7·4)	—	—	—
70—90	16·1	(14·3)	—	—	—	—	—
80—100	17·9	(16·3)	—	—	—	—	—
90—110	22·3	(20·8)	—	—	—	—	—

Times in brackets are those of the manual gearbox model, for comparison

MAXIMUM SPEEDS AND ACCELERATION TIMES

TIME IN SECONDS

¼ MILE—18·1 sec.

MAXIMUM SPEEDS		
GEAR	**m.p.h.**	**k.p.h.**
TOP (mean)	117·8	189·5
(best)	119·0	191·6
3rd:	78	126
2nd:	49	79
1st:	27	43

TIME IN SECONDS	4·6	6·1	8·4	11·4	15·1	20·0	26·9	34·9	49·2	
TRUE SPEED m.p.h.	0	30	40	50	60	70	80	90	100	110
CAR SPEEDOMETER		31	40	50	61	72	83	93	103	113

FUEL AND OIL CONSUMPTION

(see text)

Test Distance ....445 miles

Overall m.p.g....................................17·7
(15·9 litres/100 km.)

Estimated (DIN) m.p.g. ....27·5
(10·3 litres/100 km.)

Normal range m.p.g. ....18—23
(15·7—12·3 litres/100 km.)

Grade .... Premium (96—98 RM)

OIL CONSUMPTION (SAE 20) 5,000m.p.g.

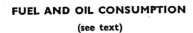

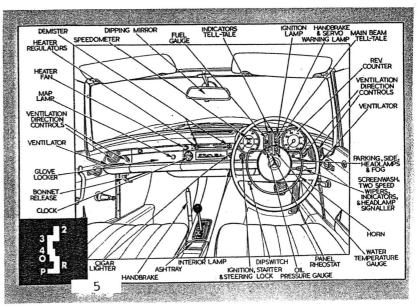

This automatic model of the 230SL was finished in dark blue which, in our opinion, suited the car better and certainly aroused more comment and envying glances than the all-white finish of the manual gearbox model previously tested.

Mercedes-Benz 230SL Automatic . . .

taken would be representative for the Roadster version as well—this model being the same as a coupé-convertible without the hardtop. With the automatic model, however, figures were taken with the rather heavy hardtop still fitted, and it may be that the performance difference between the two cars, if tested in identical trim, would be even less than that shown.

A second point is that, because of the short time it was available, the automatic model covered too few miles to compensate fully for the excessive amount of petrol which inevitably is consumed during performance testing, accounting for the rather heavy overall consumption figure of 17.7 m.p.g., compared with 22.3 for the manual gearbox model. In practice, although the automatic gearbox model is undoubtedly less economical than one with standard transmission, it is able to return about 20 m.p.g., improving to 22 on a long run.

There is only an initial difference in performance between automatic and manual versions, the automatic taking 8.4sec to 50, 11.4 to 60, and 34.9 to 100 m.p.h., compared with the manual car's 7.5, 10.7 and 34.4sec. Top speed of the automatic is 2.5 slower than the manual car's 120.3 m.p.h.

This second 230SL also featured the occasional seat fitted at the rear to carry a third occupant sideways, with feet in a well to the rear of the front passenger seat. proved acceptably comfortable for quite long distance and is an option which greatly increases the scope of the car. With hardtop or hood in position, headroom is adequate for an adult of average height.

The third option on the car was dealt with in the previous test—the excellent power assistance which makes the steering delightfully light without introducing any of the weaknesses of inaccuracy or too-lively response. It is completely unobtrusive and there are no side effects to tell a newcomer to the 230SL that the lightness of the steering is due to power assistance. Of the transmission, too, no better car could be picked to persuade the most ardent diehard to surrender his allegiance to the old concept of clutch and gear shift.

Left: The automatic selector lever is shorter than the manual gear stick, and runs in a nylon-lined gate.   Right: An occasional seat is available at extra cost, and is upholstered in leather or Vynide.   It affords reasonable comfort for an adult to travel in the back for quite long journeys

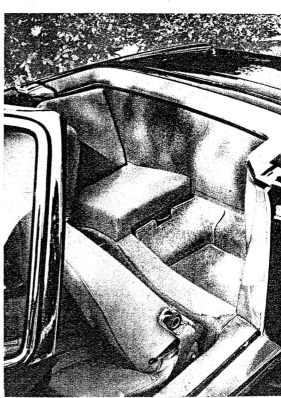

6

One of our editors had, as his first imported car, a liberated Mercedes-Benz convertible of about 1934 vintage. It had a six-cylinder flathead engine, wooden dash, five forward speeds and twin, side-mounted spare tires. His bit of intelligence is unrelated to this 230-SL road test in any way, except that he finds a number of remarkable similarities between that car and this new one.

This is a fact about Mercedes-Benz cars that is absolutely unique in our automotive experience—that there is a Mercedes-Benz *personality* that is immediately apparent in every model they build, indeed in every model they've built since they went to swing axle rear suspension in 1931. Something about the sound and the way you sit would give the car's identity away, even if you were blindfolded.

We should have expected this in the 230-SL, but nonetheless it came as a surprise. This is either the most substantial solid light car, or the quickest most agile heavy car we have ever driven. The driving sensation, particularly as related to the seat design with its almost chair-height, and the angle of the steering wheel, are exactly like the Mercedes sports coupes—the 220-SE and 300-SE. The only important difference is that the 230-SL feels very tiny, and *very* fast. The driver's impression is kind of whimsical—as though a big, plush Mercedes touring car had been touched with a magic wand and transformed into a lithe, impatient thoroughbred without losing any of its town car-respectability.

Nearly every one of the car's beautifully crafted components is either the same as, or similar in design to its counterpart on the sedans. Basic engine, suspension, brakes, interior appointments, switches and gauges are all common to other cars in the M-B line up. The single pertinent exception is the new direct-port fuel injection and cylinder head. Compression ratio is higher than on the 220-SE (9.3 vs 8.7) along with larger valves and a hotter camshaft. Unlike the older car's manifold injection system, this new Bosch unit employs a pump with six separate plungers and individual pipes running to the injectors, which are screwed into the cylinder head. This method allows preheating of the mixture passing through the head and takes advantage of the turbulence in the intake port to facilitate complete and rapid vaporization.

This engine has flexibility equal to the 220- and 300-SE powerplants, but

CAR and DRIVER ROAD TEST

Mercedes Benz 230-SL

MERCEDES-BENZ 230-SL

Importer: Mercedes-Benz Sales, Inc.,
635 South Main Street
South Bend 27, Indiana

Price as tested: $7980 East Coast POE

ACCELERATION

Zero to	Seconds
30 mph	3.1
40 mph	5.0
50 mph	6.9
60 mph	9.9
70 mph	12.0
80 mph	15.0
90 mph	18.9
100 mph	22.0
Standing ¼ mile	17.0 @ 86 mph

Top Speed:
125 mph
(estimated)

Standing ¼-mile

MERCEDES-BENZ 230 SL
Temperature .... 57° F
Wind velocity .... 14 mph
Altitude above sea level 1100 ft
Test weight .... 3000 lbs
In 4 runs, 0-60 mph times varied between 9.9 and 10.2 seconds

ACCELERATION TIME-SECONDS

ENGINE

Water-cooled in-line six, cast iron block, 7 main bearings
Bore x stroke ....3.23 x 2.87 in, 82 x 72.8 mm
Displacement ....141 cu in, 2306 cc
Compression ratio ....9.3 to one
Carburetion ....Daimler-Benz/Bosch fuel injection system
Valve gear ....Single overhead camshaft with finger followers
Power (SAE) ....170 bhp @ 5600 rpm
Torque ....159 lb-ft @ 4500 rpm
Specific power output ....1.21 bhp per cu in, 73.8 bhp per liter
Usable range of engine speeds ....500-6500 rpm
Electrical system ......12-volt, 63 amp-hr battery
Fuel recommended ....Premium
Mileage ....16-24 mpg
Range on 17.2-gallon tank: ....275-410 miles

DRIVE TRAIN

Clutch ....9-inch single dry plate
Transmission ....4-speed all-synchro

Gear	Ratio	Over-all	mph/1000 rpm	Max mph
Rev	3.92	14.68	-5.0	-32.5
1st	4.42	16.60	4.5	29.3
2nd	2.28	8.58	8.7	56.8
3rd	1.53	5.72	12.9	86.0
4th	1.00	3.75	19.7	125.0

Final drive ratio ....3.75 to one

CHASSIS

Unit-construction, all-steel structure.
Wheelbase ....94.5 in
Track ....F 58.5, R 58.5 in
Length ....169 in
Width ....69.2 in
Height ....51.5 in
Ground clearance ....5.4 in
Curb weight ....2855 lbs
Test weight ....3000 lbs
Weight distribution front/rear % 52.5/47.5
Pounds per bhp (test weight) 17.65
Suspension: F: Ind., wishbones and coil springs, anti-roll bar.
R: Ind., single-joint, low-pivot-point swing axles, vertical coil springs and trailing arms, auxiliary transverse coil spring.
Brakes ....10-in Girling discs front, 9-in Alfin drums rear, 351 sq in swept area
Steering ....Recirculating ball
Turns lock to lock 3½
Turning circle ....33.5 ft
Tires ....185 x 14
Revs per mile 817

the valve timing is such that power can be felt coming in with a great, powerful push at around 4000 rpm. The sensation is particularly gratifying in first and second gears, but is no less obvious in third and fourth. This engine is meant to wind, and wind it does! The neophyte driver is invariably disappointed in the 230-SL's performance because, in his initial uncertainty, he's unwilling to run the engine in the upper reaches of the rpm range. Once he gets over this understandable inhibition he finds that the car is fast enough for all but the most jaded, super-stock-dulled palate. Mercedes' approach on all of their recent high-speed touring designs has been to use a much shorter final drive ratio and to cruise the engine at relatively high revs. This is particularly evident to the driver who finds himself in a Mercedes after driving an American car or one of the English or continental cars fitted with overdrive. On a long trip, the man unfamiliar with the car is apt to be a little concerned about turning 4000 to cruise at less than eighty miles per hour. The presence of another 2500 useful revs is quite reassuring, and it soon seems like the most natural thing in the world to see the tach needle pointed well into the higher numbers.

The extreme responsiveness of the engine between 4000 and 6500 rpm is a contributing factor to the 230-SL's fantastic stability on twisty, enthusiast-travelled roads. The car is so completely straightforward and comfortable in maximum-speed handling situations that we were led to experiment endlessly with various combinations of brakes, steering, throttle opening, and line. Many times we'd enter a corner at what seemed like a very courageous speed, only to find ourselves coming out twenty-five mph faster at the other end, and feeling very silly about hav-

Imagine your hands on that steering wheel with the tachometer at 5000 and the speedometer at 100—you'll be in Nice in an hour.

ing slowed down at all. Due to the car's perfect balance and dead-accurate steering—plus the presence of Mr. Dunlop's fantastic SP braced-tread tires—there is no need for any fancy nonsense about setting it up, or hanging the tail out. The car's cornering power is so high that one simply goes roaring into the turn, chooses his line, steers, and opens the throttle to taste. The result is a smoothly negotiated corner that will make your passenger think you're a virtuoso, and drivers of other cars wish that they had taken the bus.

All this over-the-road goodness can be attributed directly to Mercedes' brilliant engineer-driver Rudolf Uhlenhaut and his belief that the car's entire chassis/suspension configuration should be directly related to the ride, stability and adhesive characteristics of the tire to be used. We have driven lots of cars that were materially improved by changing to a belted tire (i.e. Michelin X, Pirelli Cinturato, Continental Radial, or Dunlop SP), but we had never driven a car—like the 230-SL—that was specifically designed to take advantage of their unique and beneficial qualities. This combination of absolute security, complete stability, and plain old hell-raising fun must be driven to be believed.

Since we mentioned security, perhaps we ought to touch briefly on that aspect of the 230-SL. The wife of our editor/publisher has spent nearly ten years being subjected to hell-for-leather cross-country trips and week-end jaunts in the widest variety of cars imaginable. She can weather virtually any kind of automotive adventure without complaint, but she is unnerved by on-the-limit driving in very fast cars. En route from New York City to Watkins Glen, for the U.S. GP, she was whisked over unknown roads, in the rain, at speeds faster than she had ever experienced,

and she never interrupted her knitting or caught her breath in that sharp gasp so common to enthusiasts' wives in moments of panic. The car is so quiet, and so steady, that the highest possible touring speeds seem completely relaxed and leisurely. This feature alone should attract thousands of frustrated Nuvolaris whose wives' discomfort tends to put an upper limit on the speed from point A to point B.

The 230-SL's imparted feeling of security stems from more than its well-mated chasis, suspension and tires, and excellent brakes—it is a Mercedes, and is thus put together well. For such a sporting proposition, it is very luxurious as we pointed out at the beginning, the cockpit appointments were lifted almost intact from the 220-SE) and remarkably quiet. There appears to be no discernable difference in workmanship, weather protection, quality of materials, or panel fit between this newest Mercedes GT car and any luxury car in the M-B line, short of the new 600 limousine (West Germany's alternative to an independent nuclear deterrent). Readers at this point will snort that any cottonpicking car that costs eight grand *should* be well-finished and properly put together. To those innocents we can only say that there are large numbers of unscrupulous Englishmen and Europeans asking $7500 and up, for cars that aren't even in the same league with our test car. All this comfort creature and luxury serves to underline and emphasize a basic truth that is dawning on American enthusiasts—that is, you needn't be uncomfortable to go fast.

Our test was conducted using the hard-top version of the 230-SL with standard four-speed transmission, manual steering, Girling disc front brakes and Alfin drums at the rear. The brakes are power assisted by an Ate hydraulic booster unit (Ate, interestingly enough,

is a Dunlop licensee and is thus a direct competitor of Girling). Power-assisted steering is available as an option, as is Mercedes' very popular automatic transmission. We prefer the car as we tested it, without the luxury power-assists, but a burgeoning share of the Mercedes market will disagree with us. There are a lot of self-indulgent burghers who buy cars like the 230-SL for the same reasons that they buy Countess Mara neckties—because everybody knows they're expensive. Customers of this ilk are not apt to respond to the joys of gear shifting. We're just as happy they don't.

In designing the body for the 230-SL, Dr. Wilfert, Daimler-Benz's chief stylist, succeeded in creating a modern sports car shape which does not cling too closely to the precepts laid down by Pininfarina and Michelotti, who virtually dictate body design all over Europe. The lines are crisp and clean, and lend themselves well to good space utilization, as well as offering a good view from inside.

The 230-SL has been criticized by a few people, mostly on its appearance or because it is too expensive adequately to replace the 190-SL and not fast enough to replace the 300-SL, both of which were discontinued when the 230-SL was introduced. We disagree on both counts. Just as Mercedes broke new ground in car design with the gull-wing, 300-SL coupe, so have they with this car. We predict that several 230-SL styling features will appear on new cars in the near future. As to the suitability of the 230-SL to replace the 190- and 300-SL roadsters, we can only opine that both of the now-defunct models were out-of-date and overpriced. This tough but oh-so-gentle newcomer has made both of them—and an awful lot of other cars as well—as dead as yesterday's newspapers.

MERCEDES-BENZ 230-SL

Stuttgart's new middle-sized SL replaces both the 190-SL and the 300-SL. Neither as hot as the latter nor as cool as the former, it's a highly refined piece of GT machinery

There's something about a Mercedes-Benz. Something about *any* Mercedes-Benz, regardless of size or purpose, which telegraphs—through all the senses—the fact that it *is* a Mercedes-Benz and nothing else. If the body of the 230-SL were completely disguised, anyone familiar with Mercedes-Benz products would instantly recognize it as a member of the family the minute he drove it away. From the sound of the exhaust. From the feel and position of the seat and controls. Even from the smell of the grease, the leather, the paint. We're not sure how they do it, but we're damn sure they do.

One by one, each basic model in the Mercedes-Benz line has been upgraded. The first to receive the treatment was the six-cylinder sedan group, then the four-cylinder sedan group, and now—after years of speculation—a new sports model. Rumor had it that the new car would be an addition to the sports-car line-up, a cut above the 190-SL (*September '58 C/D*), but along with the 230-SL's unveiling at the Geneva Show came word that the 190-SL and the 300-SL—oldest cars in the Mercedes-Benz stable—have been discontinued.

After a little reflection, this makes good sense. What purpose would be served in continuing or revamping the older SLs when the 230-SL—falling in an untapped median area between the two—has a wider appeal than both of its predecessors combined? The 230-SL might even steal some sales from the 220-SE coupé (*August '62 C/D*), a posh boulevard job much in vogue with the wealthy just now.

Yet the 230-SL is closer in design concept to the 190-SL and the 220-SE coupé (which provide the running gear and engine, respectively) than to the 300-SL (*December '57 C/D*), a car which was originally spawned as an out-and-out competition machine; the 230-SL is much longer on creature comfort and an image of status rather than sport.

As may be seen in the comparison chart on page 56, all the SL-series cars have a 94.5-inch wheelbase and the 230-SL is really as "wide-track" as its looks—the front track is four inches wider than that of the 300-SL.

The S in SL, by the way, means *Super*; the L means *Leicht* (light, as in weight) and the E in 220-SE means *Einspritz*, an onomatopoetic word for fuel injection. We'll go along with the S; the 230-SL has a bored-out and souped-up version of the already-warm six-cylinder 220-SE engine. Compared with the 190-SL's four-cylinder engine, the 230-SL delivers 50 more bhp at a weight penalty—for the whole car—of only 55 pounds. But we

can't help feeling that a 170-bhp car that weighs over 2,800 pounds hardly merits the designation *Leicht.*

The 230-SL engine is quite a nice piece of work. The bore is only .079 inches more than the 220-SE's, but the extra 36 bhp comes from more than an increase of 111 cc. The cylinder head is completely new, with a higher compression ratio (9.3 vs. 8.7) and larger valves in addition to a slightly modified camshaft. Instead of the two-plunger Bosch injection pump of the 220-SE with its three distribution units, the Bosch pump on the 230-SL has six separate plungers and individual pipes direct to each injector. Unlike the Mercedes/Bosch system used on the 220-SE engine, injection does not take place in the intake manifold; the nozzles are screwed into the cylinder head itself, emerging quite close to the valve. This method pre-heats the mixture as it passes through the head and takes advantage of the turbulence occurring in the intake port to obtain complete and rapid vaporization.

By way of further comparison, the 190-SL has the much-maligned double Solex 44-PHH side-draft carburetors and the 300-SL has a Bosch injection system with the nozzles screwed directly into the cylinder walls where they are shrouded by the pistons at TDC. The earliest 300-SL prototypes had Solex carbs and the straight-eight (actually, double-four) M-196 engines, as used in the 300-SLR and Grand Prix cars, had direct Bosch injection with either curved or straight plenum chambers, the so-called "ram" tubes.

The ram-tube configuration for the 230-SL was determined after typically Teutonic, exhaustive experimentation with tubes of differing diameters, angles and lengths. Rudolf Uhlenhaut, the man responsible for such

developments, feels that the moderate length of the 230-SL ram tubes is the optimum compromise between low-end torque and top-end power, with little room for improvement either way. The acceleration figures, falling between those of the 220-SE coupé and the 300-SL, bear him out and, for our part, we discovered that the car will accelerate smoothly in any gear but top from 500 rpm to well beyond the red-line, making a tachometer a categorical imperative in this car. Luckily, it's standard equipment.

The mixture and strength of the incoming fuel charge is controlled by a governor connected to the throttle and sensors of engine speed, intake air pressure and water temperature. There is no choke *per se,* but as in most road-going fuel-injection systems, there is an automatic cold-start and warm-up enricher.

Along with development of fuel injection, Engineer Uhlenhaut devoted a great deal of time and attention to the exhaust valves. As a result of another almost-endless series of tests, Uhlenhaut formulated a number of theories which, in his opinion, pertain to all high-performance engines.

Applying Uhlenhaut's findings to the 230-SL engine, Mercedes-Benz came up with the following: the exhaust valves are sodium-cooled and made from an alloy high in nickel content, the stems are chrome-plated and the guides are of bronze to aid heat dispersal, the seats are "armored" and an automatic device rotates the valve in relation to its seat every time it is opened. Wow!

In common with all Mercedes-Benz passenger-car engines since 1951, the in-line valves are operated by a single overhead camshaft with a finger interposed between the valve and the cam lobe. This provides a minimum of friction, weight and noise throughout the speed range. In the 230-SL, the intake-valve diameter is 1.47 inches and the lift is .245 inches.

The cylinder head is light alloy while the block remains cast iron, as on the 220 series engines. The large and complex injected engine completely fills the front bay of the 230-SL, but is located far enough forward that it does not intrude upon the foot-room of the passenger compartment.

The car's cornering power is unusually high, but, with a nose-heavy weight distribution (52.5% on the front wheels) and a "sticky" rear suspension, there is quite a bit of built-in understeer which Mercedes-Benz likes to think of as a safety factor: if you close the throttle in the middle of a turn, there is a smooth transition to what feels like a neutral steering condition. It's all very stable—you simply steer your way around the turn until you feel like applying power again.

Somewhat surprisingly, opening the throttle wide in a turn will increase the understeer, though not to the extent that the front end plows. Steering with the throttle, i.e., utilizing the variable slip-angles of the Continental Radial tires, thus becomes a highly practicable cornering method, obviating the necessity for anything as Wagnerian as a four-wheel drift.

As the center of gravity of the 230-SL is located about 16.5 inches above the ground, the front anti-sway bar does not have to work terribly hard at keeping the car level in corners. The driver, in fact, feels no roll at all, but spectators do note a definite lean.

The front roll center is only 4.82 inches above ground level, while the low-pivot, single-joint swing axle rear end (pioneered by Mercedes-Benz in 1951) has its roll center at 8.45 inches. There is no anti-sway bar at the rear, as the Mercedes-Benz system has much the same roll stiffness as a normal rigid-axle layout. In addition to the coil springs taking vertical loads from the rear axles, there is an auxiliary horizontal coil spring behind the differential carrier coupled to both axle halves which resists large vertical axle movements while allowing a lower roll couple—the same effect Porsche achieves with a transverse "camber compensator" leaf spring.

Wheel travel is normal for a sports-touring car; in compression, the front springs allow 4.55 inches and the rear springs 4.10 inches. On rebound, front wheel travel

New 230-SL (right) shows seven years' advance in design over

is 3.75 inches and the rear wheels 5.25 inches. The normal rear-wheel camber setting is slightly negative; it is only on severe rebound that the camber becomes positive enough to materially affect the 230-SL's handling characteristics.

The steering box is the recirculating-ball type; the linkage has the well-known Mercedes-Benz shock absorber which reduces or eliminates road shock transmitted to the steering wheel. As on the 220-SE, some muscular effort is required for hairpin turns and parking maneuvers. For the not-so-sporty, there is a power steering option. Don't sneer; this is the same praiseworthy item we noted in our road test of the 300-SE (*January '63 C/D*) which always retains feel of the road and requires purposeful effort—not like the overpowered versions so prevalent over here. True, there is less feed-back than with manual steering, but there's enough to give the driver a pretty fair idea of how much "tiger" he is unleashing on the corner.

The power steering has a slightly quicker ratio (three vs. three-and-a-half turns lock to lock), so you have to alter your methods when going from one system to another. With manual steering, you normally set the car up for the corner with a fast flick of the wheel, to over-

ENGINE	190-SL	220-SE Coupé	230-SL	300-SL
Type and Induction	4-cyl sohc, 2 Solex	6-cyl sohc, port FI	6-cyl sohc, port FI	6-cyl sohc, direct FI
Displacement	116 cu in, 1,897 cc	134 cu in, 2,195 cc	141 cu in, 2,306 cc	183 cu in, 2,996 cc
Bore and Stroke (in.)	3.34 x 3.30	3.26 x 2.87	3.23 x 2.87	3.35 x 3.46
Compression ratio	8.5:1	8.7:1	9.3:1	9.5:1
Bhp @ rpm	120 @ 5,700	134 @ 5,000	170 @ 5,600	250 @ 6,200
Torque (lb.-ft.) @ rpm	107 @ 2,800	152 @ 4,100	159 @ 4,500	228 @ 5,000
CHASSIS				
Wheelbase	94.5 in	108.25	94.5	94.5
Track, F and R	56.0/56.0 in	58.5/58.5	58.5/58.5	54.5/56.5
Length	166 in	192	168.7	180.0
Weight	2,800 lbs	3,224	2,855	3,100
% on drive wheels	N.A.	47	47.5	52.0
PERFORMANCE				
0-30	4.9 sec	4.0	3.8	2.7
0-60	13.7	12.7	10.1	7.8
0-90	N.A.	31.6	19.2	15.4
Standing ¼ @ mph	20.1 sec @ 75	19.2 @ 73	17.0 @ 85	16.3 @ 91
DRIVE TRAIN				
MPH (ratio) in gears				
I	31 (3.52)	28 (3.64)	29 (4.42)	38 (3.34)
II	47 (2.32)	44 (2.36)	57 (2.28)	63 (1.97)
III	75 (1.52)	72 (1.53)	85 (1.53)	90 (1.39)
IV (over-all)	109 (3.89)	106 (4.10)	125 (3.75)	136 (3.89)
PRICE (approx.)	$5,200	$8,800	$8,000	$11,100

come the initial understeer. With the power assist, you begin as early, but put less lock on the wheels at first—then more and more as you go deeper into the turn and ease off lock just as leisurely at the apex.

Some years back there was a big row when a well-known and well-fixed sports-car driver-patron tried to order a Mercedes-Benz with a floor shift (not, of course, an SL model). He was informed, as he was escorted from the M-B showroom, that Mercedes-Benz did not consider a floor shift proper attire for a touring car. At some point since, Mercedes-Benz got the message; now both the 220-SE coupé and the 230-SL have "four on the floor;" a lovely, all-synchromesh transmission which has only two counts against it. One—though the placing of the shift lever is ideal, the shift itself is a little vague in its gate, just as all German floor shifts of recent years have been. Two—the ratios are a mixed bag indeed (*see comparison chart*).

First gear (4.42) is very short and runs the engine out of revs at 30 mph; it is only the marvelous flexibility of the engine that prevents a dying gasp as second gear (2.28) is engaged. The drop from second to third (1.53) is well spaced, but while third is good to over 80 mph, there is an annoying gap between it and fourth. Mercedes-Benz might argue that a close-ratio gearbox isn't necessary with an engine of the 230-SL's low-speed pulling power (though the torque doesn't peak till 4,500 rpm) but we would counter that it is precisely because of such an engine that a close-ratio gearbox is at its best —sporty, fun and easier on the powerplant and drive train—if not on the clutch.

There is an automatic-transmission option for the 230-SL; the same well-designed, well-built unit described in the December '61 C/D, featuring a hydraulic coupling and a four-speed planetary gearbox of light weight and compact dimension (just three inches longer and 30 pounds heavier than the manual transmission). It, too, is controlled by a floor-mounted lever, moving through a staggered quadrant (2-3-4-0-R-P, reading front to rear). By using the stick to hold the engine to the red-line (5,600 rpm) in each gear, the acceleration is almost as good as with the manual transmission and the difference in top speed is only three mph (121 vs. 124). The ratios are unchanged from those of the 300-SE (or the 220 and 190 series, for which this transmission has now been made optional), with a 3.98 first gear, a 2.52 second, a 1.52 third and direct fourth. Obviously inspired by the GM HydraMatic, the Daimler-Benz

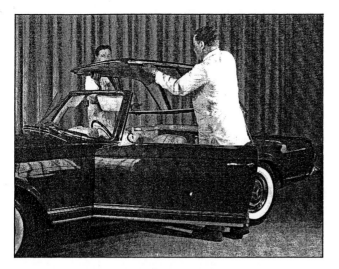

Low belt line, slim pillars and slightly dished roof give the 230-SL hardtop distinctly modern styling which may kick off a trend.

Road Research Report
Mercedes-Benz 230-SL

Importer: Mercedes-Benz Sales, Inc.
635 South Main Street
South Bend 27, Indiana

No. of U.S. Dealers: 343

Planned annual production: NA

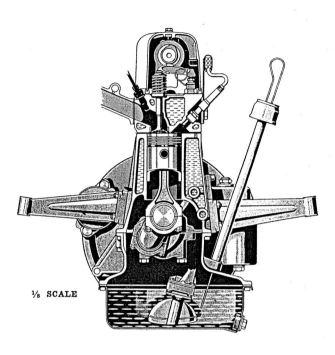

⅛ SCALE

PRICE: Approx. $8,000 P.O.E.

OPERATING SCHEDULE:

Fuel recommended.................................... Premium
Mileage.. 16-24 mpg
Range on 17.2 gallon tank........................275-410 miles
Crankcase capacity.................................5½ quarts
Change at intervals of.............................3,800 miles
Number of grease fittings..............................20
Most frequent maintenance..Oil change, lubrication and regular maintenance (factory chart C) at 3,800 miles

ENGINE:

Displacement....................................141 cu in, 2,306 cc
Dimensions.................6 cyl, 3.23-in bore, 2.87-in stroke
Valve gear.........Single overhead camshaft with finger followers
Compression ratio...................................9.3 to one
Power (SAE)....................170 bhp @ 5,600 rpm
Torque........................159 lb-ft @ 4,500 rpm
Usable range of engine speeds...............500-6,500 rpm
Carburetion...............Daimler-Benz/Bosch fuel-injection system

CHASSIS:

Wheelbase ....94.5 in
Track ....F 58.5 in, R 58.5 in
Length ....168.7 in
Ground Clearance ....5.4 in
Suspension: F: ind., wishbones and coil springs, anti-roll bar
R: ind., single-joint low-pivot swing axles, coil springs and auxiliary transverse coil spring
Steering ....Recirculating ball
Turns, lock to lock...................................3½
Turning circle diameter between curbs...................33½ ft
Tire size ....185 x 14
Pressures recommended...................F 24, R 24 psi
Brakes........10-in Girling discs front, 9-in Alfin drums rear, 351 sq in swept area
Curb weight (full tank)..........................2,855 lbs
Percentage on the driving wheels.....................47.5

DRIVE TRAIN:

Clutch.......................................Single dry plate

Gear	Synchro	Ratio	Step	Over-all	Mph per 1,000 rpm
Rev	No	3.92	—	14.68	—5.0
1st	Yes	4.42	94%	16.60	4.5
2nd	Yes	2.28	49%	8.58	8.7
3rd	Yes	1.53	53%	5.72	12.9
4th	Yes	1.00	—	3.75	19.7

Final drive ratio.................................3.75 to one

ACCELERATION:

Zero to	Seconds
30 mph	3.1
40 mph	5.0
50 mph	6.9
60 mph	9.9
70 mph	12.0
80 mph	15.0
90 mph	18.9
100 mph	22.0
Standing ¼-mile	17.0

Continental Radial

F 24 psi
R 24 psi

Steering Behavior

Wheel position to maintain 400-foot circle at speeds indicated.

Idle · Green-line · Torque · Power · Red-line

Engine Flexibility
RPM in thousands

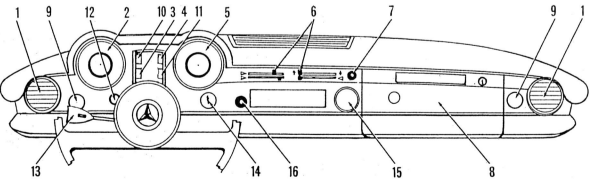

(1) Fresh-air outlet; (2) Tachometer; (3) Oil-pressure gauge; (4) Warning lights for battery charge and high beam; (5) Speedometer; (6) Heater and fresh-air controls; (7) Heater fan switch; (8) Glove compartment; (9) Heater outlet; (10) Fuel gauge; (11) Water temperature gauge; (12) Light switch; (13) Turn signal, wiper and washer, headlight flasher switch; (14) Ignition and starter; (15) Clock; (16) Cigar lighter.

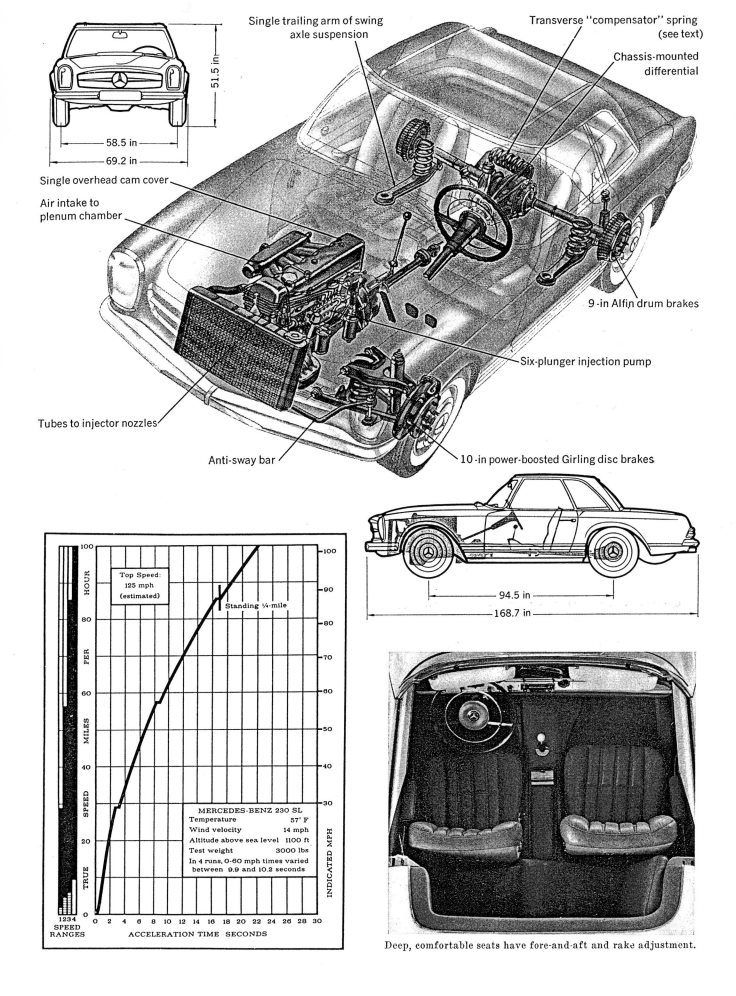

Single trailing arm of swing axle suspension

Transverse "compensator" spring (see text)

Chassis-mounted differential

51.5 in

58.5 in

69.2 in

Single overhead cam cover

Air intake to plenum chamber

9-in Alfin drum brakes

Six-plunger injection pump

Tubes to injector nozzles

Anti-sway bar

10-in power-boosted Girling disc brakes

94.5 in

168.7 in

Top Speed: 125 mph (estimated)

Standing ¼-mile

MERCEDES-BENZ 230 SL
Temperature .... 57° F
Wind velocity .... 14 mph
Altitude above sea level .... 1100 ft
Test weight .... 3000 lbs
In 4 runs, 0-60 mph times varied between 9.9 and 10.2 seconds

MILES PER HOUR

TRUE   SPEED   MILES

INDICATED MPH

1234 SPEED RANGES

ACCELERATION TIME - SECONDS

Deep, comfortable seats have fore-and-aft and rake adjustment.

15

THE MERCEDES-BENZ 230SL ~ By J. EASON GIBSON

ALTHOUGH the latest Mercedes-Benz 230SL is the high-performance model from that maker's range, it should not be compared with the earlier 300SL, with its truly startling performance. The latest model is, perhaps, better described in words rather than in mere figures, as it is its manner of performance that makes it such an outstanding car. Its comfort, refinement and general handling qualities have to be experienced to be appreciated fully. If I were asked to select a suitable car to persuade a diehard motorist that automatic transmission and power-assisted steering were worthwhile modern features I would select the 230SL: the manner in which these two features are provided sets an example other makers have not yet equalled.

The six-cylinder engine is basically similar to that used on the 220SE saloon, with a slightly greater capacity granted by an increase of 2 mm. in bore diameter. A compression ratio of 9.3 to 1 is used, and the latest six-plunger pump supplies the fuel-

The seating sets a standard that one wishes others would copy, rather than building seats that are meant to look opulent and impressive. The seats and squabs on the 230SL are correctly shaped to give both comfort and security, and the upholstery is matched to the suspension to prevent bounce over uneven surfaces. Changing the native product to right-hand drive for the British market has produced two minor irritations. The hand-brake lever is on the left-hand side of the transmission tunnel, and the master switch for the lights is rather tucked away behind the steering wheel.

A very clever lever-type switch beneath the steering wheel performs such a variety of functions that the electrician responsible for its wiring has my admiration. It operates the indicators, flashes the headlamps, works the windscreen washer, switches the wipers on and—the final refinement—it can be used to give normal or fast speed for the wipers. The wipers have an unusual overlapping action,

cornering at high speed. The power-assisted steering is the most successful I have tried. It allows the steering to be light and effortless in traffic or when parking, but not a fraction of high-speed accuracy and response has been lost. To reach the ultimate in cornering speeds it is necessary to drive the car on a racing circuit, and this indicates the amazing margin of safety that prevails under normal road conditions. The driver never needs to worry about the reactions of his passenger: the lack of roll and the excellently shaped seats allow the latter to relax completely. So outstandingly good are the brakes and so helpful is the servo-assistance that some experience with the car is needed to avoid a tendency to over-brake on occasion. Only fractionally more effort than that needed to work the average clutch pedal gives a braking figure better than the theoretical maximum, and the efficiency does not diminish with repeated severe use.

A particularly attractive feature of the car, and one that would encourage an owner from the long-term point of view, is the outstanding rigidity and obvious strength of the construction. One gains the justifiable impression that it could be driven all day at maximum speed over the worst of *pavé* surfaces. The comfort of both driver and passenger are assisted on long trips by a complete and easily controlled ventilation system, one portion of which demists the windscreen and also the side windows. The petrol consumption throughout my test averaged exactly 20 m.p.g., but I am convinced that this is the worst figure anyone could expect, and it was no doubt contributed to by my very enthusiastic driving. I am confident that in average use the figure would be between 23 and 25 m.p.g. With a tank capacity of 14.3 gallons—lacking a reserve, unfortunately—a range of around 300 miles is possible between fuel stops.

Just as some people prefer craftsman-built furniture to the "orange-box" type, so there are motorists who obtain pleasure from driving a car that is a good piece of engineering. For such motorists the 230SL will exert a special appeal. With the exception of the handbrake lever and the headlamp switch I have already mentioned, I found the car faultless.

I would describe the 230SL as one of the safest of fast cars for the relatively inexperienced driver, and this is due to the exceptional road-holding and cornering, the qualities of the power-assisted steering and the excellent brakes.

"An amazing margin of safety prevails under normal road conditions"

of 150 brake horse power is delivered at 5,000 r.p.m., but the fact that maximum torque is delivered at 4,500 r.p.m. indicates that the lower gears are intended to be used. With fuel injection instead of carburettors there is no need for a choke; instead, an automatic enrichment device delivers extra fuel for a cold start. At all other times the injection system delivers the correct mixture for temperature and atmospheric conditions, thus preventing loss of power at high altitudes. The use of fuel injection and the separate header tank for the cooling system make the engine compartment rather crowded, but the main components are all easily reached for maintenance.

The car is of integral construction and gives the feeling of truly unusual rigidity in use. The suspension is independent all round, that at the front being by coil springs and wishbones and at the rear by low-pivot swing axles and coil springs. The suspension at the front is assisted by an anti-roll bar and at the rear by a compensating spring. Bilstein hydraulic telescopic dampers are used all round. The front brakes are of disc-type, with drums at the rear; and ATE servo-assistance is provided. There are independent hydraulic circuits for the front and rear brakes. The steering requires 3.6 turns of the wheel to change from lock to lock. One outmoded feature of the car is that there are 20 points requiring attention with the grease gun at intervals of 2,000 miles.

The low waistline and the high roof result in exceptionally good all-round visibility.

There is a seat for a third person sitting sideways; this can be used comfortably by an adult of just below average height. The luggage boot is very roomy and easily capable of holding the holiday load of the most sybaritic of drivers.

The over-riding manual control of the automatic transmission (which, it should be stressed, is built by the manufacturers themselves and not bought in as a proprietary part) operates in a nylon-bushed quadrant, and its smooth operation is symptomatic of the whole car. None other that I have used equals it. For the first few miles after taking over the car I literally played with this control. If placed in 4, the automatic transmission does everything for one; if placed in 3 or 2, the transmission will not change above the gear selected; and in 2, all starts are done in 1st gear. Kickdown is, of course, available whenever needed for maximum acceleration. After some experience it is possible to have the best of both worlds by combining manual control and automatism for varying traffic conditions. A change down from 4th to 3rd can be obtained with no more than finger pressure, and this gives engine braking into a corner, as well as making maximum acceleration instantly available.

The Firestone Phoenix tyres fitted to the car tested undoubtedly contributed to the car's excellent adhesion under all conditions. The all-independent suspension gives remarkable road-holding. The car is superbly balanced and there is no apparent roll when one is

THE MERCEDES-BENZ 230SL

Concessionaires: Mercedes-Benz (GB), Brentford, Middlesex

SPECIFICATION

Price	£3,595	Brakes	Girling disc front; drum rear (power assisted)
(including PT £620)		Suspension	Independent (all round)
Cubic capacity	2,306 c.c.		
Bore and stroke			
	82 × 72·8 mm.	Wheelbase	7 ft. 10½ in.
		Track (front)	4 ft. 10½ in.
Cylinders	Six	Track (rear)	4 ft. 10½ in.
Valves	Overhead	Overall length	14 ft. 1 in.
B.h.p.	150 at 5,500 r.p.m.	Overall width	5 ft. 9½ in.
Carburettors	Nil	Overall height	4 ft. 3½ in.
	(fuel injection)	Ground clearance	7 in.
Ignition	Coil	Turning circle	32 ft. 6 in.
Oil filter	Full-flow	Weight	26½ cwt.
1st gear	14·9 to 1	Fuel capacity	14·3 gall.
2nd gear	9·45 to 1	Oil capacity	9·7 pints
3rd gear	5·93 to 1	Water capacity	19 pints
Top gear	3·75 to 1	Tyres	Firestone Phoenix
Final drive	Hypoid bevel		185 × 14

PERFORMANCE

Acceleration		Max speed	118·5 m.p.h.
Top	3rd		
30-50 11·5 sec.	6·6 sec.	Petrol consumption	
40-60 12·0 sec.	6·4 sec.	20 m.p.g. at average	
0-60 (all gears) 11·3 sec.		speed of 50 m.p.h.	
Brakes 30 to 0 in 26 feet (101 per cent efficiency)			

MERCEDES BENZ 230 SL

M ANY an enthusiast has drooled over the Mercedes Benz 190 SL and while many will mourn its passing its successor the new 230 SL is clearly a touring/sports car to be coveted.

This two-seater roadster which made its debut at the Geneva Show is powered by a six-cylinder fuel-injected engine derived from the power unit which pushes the well-known 220 SE along so purposefully.

Characteristically low and long in its lines the 230 SL has a remarkable good range of visibility from the driver's seat. The flat design of the coupe roof or hard-top is largely responsible for this as it allows considerable depth not only in the windscreen but—almost as important—in the door windows and rear screen. In fact Mercedes claim that visibility is improved over the 190 SL by over 38 per cent. The flat roof also contributes to a much easier access, often a point of criticism with a low touring-sports car.

Bigger motor

The engine has been enlarged to 2.3 litres and the fuel injection system has been revised to inject into the intake duct in the cylinder head rather than the suction pipe. The compression ratio is raised to 9.3:1 with the result that the power output for the 230 SL is 170 b.h.p. at 5,600 r.p.m. Max. revs. are 6,500 r.p.m.

In general the chassis specification is similar to the Mercedes six-cylinder range except that the track is now wider both front and rear and the rear axle—single joint swing axle with coil springs and telescopic shock absorbers—has a reduction ratio of 3.75:1.

Performance enough?

The four-speed gearbox is centrally operated and the maximum speeds in the gears are 84 m.p.h. in third, and 56 in second. The maximum speed of the 230 SL is about 124 m.p.h.

The steering is by recirculating ball with automatic adjustment and steering shock absorbers. Servo steering is optional at extra cost. The brakes are suitably impressive being Girling discs at the front and Alfin brake drums at the rear assisted by a vacuum servo.

2·3 LITRES

170 B.H.P.

124 M.P.H. PLUS

Contoured bucket-type seats provide comfortable seating for two. These seats provide sufficient side support for hard cornering. If required a transverse occasional seat can be fitted to the rear.

Well ventilated

A variety of "extras" which are standard fitting ensure that 230 SL driver and passenger are always comfortable. Two speed windscreen wipers and electrically-powered washer looks after visibility while a heating and ventilation system can supply warm or cool fresh air as required without draughts.

An interesting feature is the system by which the stale air is removed through the roof lining and out through vents above the rear screen. Two blowers on the dashboard can be used for warm or cool air and are adjustable for both force and direction.

If you are thinking of having a new garage built for your 230 SL its vital statistics are length, 14ft. 1½in.; width, 5ft. 9¼in.; height, 4ft. 3½in.; weight, 2,855 lb.; fuel capacity, 14¼ gallons with a reserve of 1½ gallons. The turning circle is 33¼ft.

The United Kingdom price of the new Mercedes-Benz 230 SL is **Roadster** (basic price £2,825) including purchase tax £3,414 2s. 1d. **Coupe** (£2,865) £3,462 8s. 9d.

THE
MERCEDES-BENZ
230SL

IN 1959, during a visit to the Daimler-Benz factories at Stuttgart and Sindelfingen, I was able to enjoy a drive to Frankfurt and Koblenz in a Mercedes-Benz 190SL, and to sample this sporting Mercedes-Benz round the Nurburgring, before going on to Dusseldorf, Hanover and Bremen, then returning to Stuttgart in this fine motor car. The impression lingers of a beautifully appointed, very comfortable, essentially predictable fast car.

However, time marches on, car performance improves, and the 190SL became out-moded, so Daimler-Benz introduced the 230SL, using a modified version of the well-established 220SE fuel-injection six-cylinder overhead-camshaft power unit. By increasing the bore-diameter 2 mm., to 82 mm., using a six-plunger instead of a two-plunger Bosch injection pump, and raising the c.r. to 9.3-to-1, a power output of 150 b.h.p. is obtained at 5,500 r.p.m. and the engine runs safely to 6,500 r.p.m., giving 159 lb./ft. torque at 4,500 r.p.m.

This fine and complicated looking power unit in a typical Mercedes-Benz, with coil-spring and wishbone i.f.s., low-pivot swing-axle coil-spring i.r.s., Girling disc front and Alfin-drum rear brakes with ATE servo assistance, and a very stylish, low two-seater body having the concave-top hard-top, adds up to an extremely handsome and effortlessly fast sporting car, which, on the road, provides a great deal of satisfaction tempered with some disillusionment.

The interior exudes the quality and convenience one expects from a Mercedes-Benz. The big separate ventilated leather-upholstered seats (this leather costing an extra £151) have reclining squabs and are amongst the most comfortable I have sat in for a long time, although tending to hug one tightly. Unfortunately, the knob for squab-setting is uncomfortably close to the door, nor did the squab of the driver's seat always re-set accurately after having been hinged forward with the side lever to give access to the rear compartment, which is more fitted for canines than humans, leg room being restricted. A transverse seat can be supplied for this shelf if required, and presumably customers who order it have their legs amputated free of charge. . . .

Although Mercedes-Benz have a specialist wood-working shop for producing finely-veneered fillets and cappings, they prefer not to endow their cars with weighty wooden facias, and on the 230SL such woodwork is used merely to trim a metal facia, shallow in itself and well provided with crash padding. The centre of the steering wheel and the sun-vizors are also padded.

With the hard-top in place there is all the comfort of a fixed-head coupé with extremely good visibility through the generous window area. Six turns are needed to fully open the driver's window. The driver is confronted with a big, somewhat slippery wheel with half horn-ring, and hooded instrumentation, comprising a 140-m.p.h. Vdo speedometer (possessing total and trip odometers, the figures of the latter difficult to read, and the first one flanked by the speedometer needle when stationary) and a Vdo tachometer

recording to 7,000 r.p.m., with a red blob at 6,600 r.p.m., these dials having between them an instrument cluster containing a fuel gauge (labelled " Tank ") calibrated 4/4, 2/4, 0, with a warning light at R, and oil gauge below this calibrated 0, 15, 30, 45, its needle remaining habitually on the upper stop when the engine was running, and, in the matching panel, a trio of warning lamps above a thermometer going to 250°F but normally showing just under 180°F. A small knob at the base of this Vdo panel provides rheostat variation of facia illumination.

The facia is otherwise uncluttered. It has adjustable fresh-air vents and aircraft-style smaller vents at each end, air-flow being shut off and controlled by horizontal-quadrant levers. Discreet knobs operate the very quiet heater-fan speed adjustment, cigar lighter, and map light, and a tiny turn-button for the lamps, is set too far under the steering wheel. There is an accurate Vdo clock. The heater controls in two quadrants occupy the facia centre, over the " 230SL " insignia, the turn-indicator warning lights are at the top of the central instrument cluster, and a r.h. stalk combines the functions of operating the turn-indicators, flashing the headlamps, and putting on the wipers (but depressing its knob) and washers (by pushing the stalk down), a button on top of the knob providing for the 2-speeds of the wipers. Very handy, and not quite so complicated as it sounds !

The hand-brake lever is somewhat inaccessible on the n/s. of the transmission tunnel, on which there is an open, wood parcels' container, with lidded ash-tray in front of it. Rigid grab handles are provided on roof and doors, typically neat Mercedes flush-fitting pull-out internal door handles are used, with equally neat door-locks, there are sensibly-shaped arm-rests-cum-" pulls," big rigid pockets on the doors, the side windows are devoid of ¼-lights yet can be opened without creating any draught, big grips provide for easy fore-and-aft seat adjustment, and the hard-top is released and the hood exposed by operating a series of levers within the car. The hood is effective and free from drumming. The cubby-hole is lockable but wouldn't take a Rolleiflex camera. Its lid incorporates interior and exterior-map lamps.

Equipment embraces an anti-dazzle mirror, effective two-position roller door " keeps," foot dipper, Bosch lamps and electrics, treadle accelerator and a brake pedal of conventional size. Although the boot contains the spare wheel, it is of shallow but very generous dimensions and the lid, self-supporting, has its own key. The rear-hinged bonnet is also self-supporting, to reveal some truly impressive machinery. I missed the three-pointed star riding in front of the driver, which is not present on the 230SL.

The car submitted for test by the British concessionaires was the automatic transmission version, with optional power steering. The gear-change is effected by a little central lever moving forward through an irregular, nylon-edged gate in P,R,O,4,3,2 order. There is the usual kick-down on the accelerator, very positive, and providing impressive acceleration, with a considerable increase in

18

The luxurious seating and facia layout of the Mercedes-Benz 230SL. Note the external mirror, adjustable seat squab with release lever, neat internal door handle and lock, and conventional gear lever to actuate the automatic gearbox.

engine noise. The lever can be pushed instantly into " 3," or " 2," when these gears are held and a change-up in the normal manner is called for when 6,500 r.p.m. is reached; in " 2 " bottom gear is selected for starting, when in " 3 " the car gets off in second unless kick-down is used.

Although this easy selection and hold of the lower gears is admirable, the lever moves very readily and if pulled back quickly as maximum engine speed is reached it is possible to inadvertently go into neutral, or to get " 2 " instead of the intended " 3 " when pushing the lever forward. Normal motoring is better done in " 4," using the hold positions only when really trying, or to prevent hunting in traffic driving. An unusual feature is that the engine can be started with the lever in " P," as well as in " O." The throttle setting on the test car gave too much creep.

For high-speed driving this 230SL is effortless, predictable and stops well. It does everything very nicely indeed, in a rather characterless manner. Cornering is virtually neutral, and the steering is sensitive in spite of the power assistance, the wheel needing three turns, lock-to-lock, with only a few inches of lost

The impressive six-cylinder fuel-injection engine of the 230SL.

THE MERCEDES- BENZ 230SL
COUPE-CONVERTIBLE

Engine : Six cylinders, 82 × 72.8 mm. (2,306 c.c.). Overhead valves, operated by an overhead camshaft. 9.3 to 1 c.r. 150 (net) b.h.p. at 5,500 r.p.m.

Gear ratios : (Automatic) First, 14.9—16.6 to 1; second, 9.45—8.56 to 1; third, 5.93—5.75 to 1; top, 3.75 to 1.

Tyres : 185 × 14 Firestone Phoenix, on bolt-on steel disc wheels.

Weight : 26.3 cwt. (kerb weight).

Steering ratio : (Power steering) : 3-turns, lock-to-lock.

Fuel capacity : 14.3 gallons. (Range : approx. 286 miles).

Wheelbase : 7 ft. 10½ in.

Track : 4 ft. 10½ in.

Dimensions : 14 ft. 1 in. × 5 ft. 9¼ in. × 4 ft. 3¾ in. (hard-top in place).

Price : £3,275 (£3,959 inclusive of p.t.).

Makers : Daimler-Benz A.G., Stuttgart-Untertürkheim, W. Germany.

Concessionaires : Mercedes-Benz (G.B.) Ltd., Great West Road, Brentford, England.

Performance Data

Acceleration :

0-30 m.p.h.	..	..	3.9 sec. (3.9 sec.)
0-40 m.p.h.	..	..	5.3 sec. (5.2 sec.)
0-50 m.p.h.	..	..	7.3 sec. (7.3 sec.)
0-60 m.p.h.	..	..	9.9 sec. (9.9 sec.)
0-70 m.p.h.	..	..	13.1 sec. (13.0 sec.)
0-80 m.p.h.	..	..	17.1 sec. (17.0 sec.)
0-90 m.p.h.	..	..	23.8 sec. (23.6 sec.)
s.s. ¼-mile	..	..	17.5 sec. (17.5 sec.)

(Best times in parentheses)

Speeds in gears : 1st, 28 m.p.h.; 2nd, 50 m.p.h.; 3rd, 78 m.p.h.; top, 120 m.p.h.

The ingenious Firestone Phoenix tyres fitted to the road-test Mercedes-Benz 230SL had protruding rubber flanges to protect rims and knave-plates from rubbing on kerbs.

The Mercedes-Benz 230SL with the hood erect.

movement. Judder and kick-back are absent, the action superbly light without being over sensitive, this being extremely good power steering. The German Firestone Phoenix tyres are specially made for the 230SL and have an ingenious rubber rim on their walls to protect the wheel knave-plates from damage on kerbs. Like most Firestones they can be made to squeal if the car is cornered close to its limit, but this means very fast indeed. This Mercedes is very stable, although rather lively suspension gives a hint of swing-axle sway if a rough surface intrudes on a corner, and the big wheels can be felt riding road undulations.

The brakes feel indecisive, even spongy, yet retard the car powerfully for light pedal pressures, and are pleasantly progressive. Except when unleashing most of its 65-per-litre horses for accelerating, the engine is very quiet. It gives a top speed of 120 m.p.h. but against the watch acceleration is not particularly impressive, a s.s. ¼-mile taking fractionally longer in this car than in a Daimler Majestic Major, for example. The figures were taken two-up, with the heavy hard-top in place. On the road, however, kick-down disposes very effectively of most of the faster saloons and sports cars and using the " hold " positions of the

gear-change, the maxima were 28, 50 and 78 m.p.h., change-ups occurring at 5,800 r.p.m.

It is interesting that, wheelspin on take-off being virtually absent, driver-skill counts for nothing, a time of 17½ seconds for the s.s. ¼-mile being obtained repeatedly and the other times being notably consistent. The speedometer was commendably accurate at all speeds up to 70 m.p.h., when it read 2 m.p.h. fast. Petrol consumption of premium fuel averaged exactly 20 m.p.g. and inspection of the accessible dip-stick, which is labelled " 220SE," showed that no oil was required after 575 miles. The fuel tank provides an absolute range of 286 miles and the reserve-light, instead of flickering uncertainly, acts as a steady reminder that fuel for only about 37 miles remains.

It was very pleasant to be in a Mercedes-Benz again, product of a company which, in my opinion, makes the best all-round touring saloons and sporting 2-seaters in the world—I have not yet driven their limousine!

It is the manner in which the 230SL runs, its impeccable finish and comprehensive specification, as much as the performance which is available, that makes this a supreme sporting car for the discerning, worth the price of £3,959 that it costs in this country, in the form tested.

* * *

After the automatic 230SL I had a couple of days with an exceedingly smart red normal model, shod with ordinary Firestone Phoenix tyres and a Blaupunkt radio with an electrically-erected aerial. It had a 4-speed manual gearbox controlled by a neat little central lever, positioned a little too far back for drivers who like to sit fairly close to the wheel, but no doubt ideal for those with long legs who adopt the full-arms-stretch position. It functions lightly, with rather long movements, but the change is notchy, somewhat spoiling the speed at which the gears are changed. The lever has no spring-loading, except that protecting reverse. This is a quiet box, with good syncromesh, giving maxima of 27, 54, 80 and 121 m.p.h. The clutch has a long-travel, but is light and smooth. The manual steering takes over 3½-turns, lock-to-lock, and while light and precise on small movements from straight ahead, it becomes tiringly heavy when making normal turns, so the very good Mercedes-Benz power steering is to be preferred. My choice would be to have the manual gearbox but power steering. The Mercedes-Benz 230SL is a magnificent motor car in either form, and the more simple version sells here for £3,668.

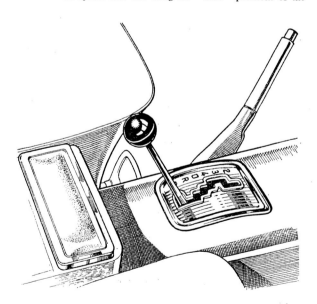

The unusual gear-gate of the 230SL.

A back-view of the eye-catching, and difficult to catch, 230SL. Its beauty is not reflected in this part of the Suffolk countryside, which is now disfigured by pylons.

MERCEDES WINS
SPA-SOFIA-LIEGE RALLY
FOR THE 2nd YEAR

OVERALL WINNERS | **BÖHRINGER & KAISER**

Driving the NEW 230SL
IN ITS FIRST EVENT!

In its first rally the new Mercedes-Benz 230SL driven by Böhringer and Kaiser was the outright winner in this severe test against top international competition. Only 22 of the 129 starters finished the arduous 3,430 mile course. Yet another victory for Mercedes-Benz in this long-distance rally, which was also won last year by Böhringer—in a Mercedes-Benz 220SE.

SUPERB AS A CAR—WITH SERVICE TO MATCH

 MERCEDES - BENZ

MERCEDES-BENZ (GREAT BRITAIN) LIMITED, GREAT WEST ROAD, BRENTFORD, MIDDLESEX
Head Office, Distribution & Service Dept. Tel. ISLeworth 2151.   Export Dept. Avenfield House, 127 Park Lane, Marble Arch, W.1. Tel. MAYfair 5578/9

A 230SL will be on view at the Motor Show on STAND 113

Concave roof of the detachable hardtop allows a great deal of headroom without detracting from the nicely-proportioned styling. A soft-top is stowed away in the rear sill, to replace the hardtop in minutes

ROAD TEST

MERCEDES-BENZ 230SL

NOT a saloon car, not a sports car, but a bit of each. It is hard to describe the Mercedes 230SL properly as it breaks entirely new ground in concept and would be difficult to emulate, but it is surely intended as a grand touring car which offers two people every possible comfort over very long distances. Even if it lacks the sheer performance that would be expected of an expensive sports car, the SL can be cruised effortlessly at 100 mph over indifferent road surfaces (and with good petrol economy if the owner is interested) to return extremely high average speeds.

The 190SL which preceded this model was always disappointing in performance, and lacked refinement with its four-cylinder engine. The 300SL, on the other hand, was smooth, tremendously fast, and rather too expensive and sophisticated for most people. The 230SL, therefore, with its six-cylinder petrol injection engine, is a go-between which combines ruggedness with lightness of control, outstanding roadholding with softness of ride, performance without drama, good looks with excellent visibility. Even without extras it costs nearly £3,500 and, as tested in Coupe-Convertible form with automatic transmission and power steering, the price is getting on for £4,000 but this heavy investment secures a superbly engineered car which should remain in first-class condition for many years.

Performances of the Mercedes-Benz range in the com-

Firestone Phoenix tyres on the 7½ in (185-15) section wheels have a generous width for the weight and performance of the 230SL, and have excellent grip on wet or dry roads

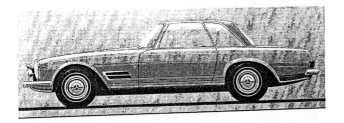

petition field are legendary, and we think particularly of participation in the most rugged rallies where the cars have proved their strength and stamina beyond doubt. Soon after the 230SL was announced, Eugen Bohringer drove one to victory in the Spa-Sofia-Liège rally, and although competition outings are rare, this was the sort of début that one would expect from the Stuttgart factory.

Throughout our test run we observed how taut and entirely rattle-free the car was, and it gave a feeling that no annoying squeaks and rattles ever would develop. The floor pressing is extremely stiff and when the body has been welded to it the structure forms a shell which is heavy but free from deflection or distortion in any circum-

stances. In appearance the 230SL is low, square-cut and purposeful with hardly any concession to a trend of flowing lines, and the Mercedes body designers have been clever in producing a line which allows extremely deep windows (and excellent headroom) without lack of proportion.

Suspension is, of course, independent all round, using coil springs and wishbones at the front and the famous low-pivot swing axles at the rear. Braking is by 10in Girling discs at the front and nine inch Alfin drums at the back, with a twin hydraulic system for safety and servo assistance for convenience. Completing the chassis description, steering is by Daimler-Benz recirculating ball mechanism with power assistance.

Refined performance

The 230SL is to other sports cars what a turbo-prop aircraft is to piston-engined varieties, although if you wish to extend the comparison to really expensive, luxury saloon cars it does not quite reach the jet-class; that would be asking too much of a well developed 2.3-litre power unit propelling nearly 26 cwt of car.

It is hard to remember at times that the engine is so relatively small, for in the intermediate gears the car accelerates very rapidly indeed—the lack of eager response above 80 mph, when top gear is engaged, may be deceptive because the 230SL does continue to gain speed up to a maximum little short of 120 mph.

The bore of the 2195 cc 220SE engine is increased by two millimetres to bring the capacity up to 2306 cc; by raising the compression ratio of the alloy head to 9.3 and tuning the Bosch injection system the power of the overhead camshaft unit is increased from 134 bhp at 5000 rpm to 170 bhp SAE (150 net) at 5600 rpm.

It might be expected that a production engine producing 65 bhp/litre would become rough or temperamental, but in fact the engine may be the most outstanding engineering achievement in that it is so smooth and quiet. The only real giveaway is in the rather poor torque at low rpm—the 144 lb ft of torque is developed at 4500 rpm, which is well up the range and precludes any scintillating performance below about 3000 rpm.

Coupled to the engine, by way of a hydraulic clutch, is a Daimler-Benz epicyclic four-speed automatic transmission which permits almost 100 per cent driver control. With the short, central lever in position 4 the car is fully automatic, starting in second gear then selecting third, and top at 30 mph on a light throttle. The kickdown at the end of the accelerator travel selects first gear briefly for quick getaway from the lights, but for top performance the driver can start in position 2, which gives the full range of bottom gear to 5700 rpm (27 mph) and then holds second until the lever is moved again. Downward changes are made very rapidly simply by pushing the lever forward in the nylon-edged gate which has serrations to prevent the selector going too far at one push.

The major criticism of the arrangement is in the selection of ratios, which are widely spaced and in fact are the same gears as in the heavier and less powerful saloons. Especially with the standard equipment manual-change versions, a close ratio box with a higher speed range in all three indirect gears would improve the SL a great deal. The standing-start performance would not be appreciably worse if the car would run to 40 mph in first, allowing corresponding increases higher up, for the car will not run beyond 68 mph in automatic third and even 80 mph on the manual hold does not seem adequate.

When parked the transmission can be locked up to supplement the handbrake, which is on the left of the transmission tunnel and too far away to be much use. The engine can be started (and the steering mechanism unlocked) only when the lever is in Park or Neutral; when a gear is selected the transmission takes up with a bump and the car has to be restrained from "creeping".

Generous boot space is reduced somewhat now that a revision places the spare wheel horizontally instead of vertically

on a dry tarmac road, but full acceleration on a damp surface will produce wheelspin right through the range of first and second gears.

When the upward changes take place at the top end of the automatic scale they are extremely smooth, but if the throttle is lifted slightly at 60 mph in third, for instance, to select top the higher ratio comes in with quite a bump and we felt that the change could be improved a lot by a driver with the manual box. At any speed within range of a lower gear, the downward change is effected immediately simply by pushing the accelerator to the floor.

Road behaviour

The steering is fairly high geared, at three turns from lock to lock, and with servo assistance it is light without being too much so, gives plenty of "feel" of the road without kickback, and in short is just about ideal. Until one is used to the car it feels almost too light as it enters fast bends, but confidence is quickly built up when the 230SL reveals no bad habits even on streaming wet roads. With the help of the 7½in section Firestone Phoenix tyres the roadholding is superb, beyond the limits of normal driving in the dry and offering a great deal of grip in the wet.

Handling is almost neutral, with just a slight bias toward understeer at high speed, but through slower corners within reach of an intermediate gear the Mercedes can be punched through with extremely controllable oversteer. Only in rare circumstances, such as bad undulations in a fast bend, can the rear axle-shafts be felt to swing, but the trait is not really alarming and is but a small penalty for the excellence of the ride.

At low speed the ride is firm, but large bumps are swallowed up by the big wheels which have a very wide track in relation to the wheelbase. Indeed, sitting in the car as it goes along one really feels that there is a wheel at each corner and it seems unlikely that a 230SL could

Gentle driving is accompanied only by a faint whine from the automatic gears; engine noise is almost entirely absent and at any speed up to 100 mph the car is exceptionally quiet, particularly when the throttle is backed off for cruising—there is hardly any wind noise either until 100 mph is exceeded.

Tramp hard on the throttle and the SL is transformed. The engine utters a subdued roar which hardens in tone as the revs go up and the acceleration is quite impressive up to around 70 mph, when the car's weight and high gearing in top combine to slow this rapid progress. But as we have indicated, there is still plenty of speed to come and the reduction in acceleration is only relative. From a standing start the rear wheels can just about squeak

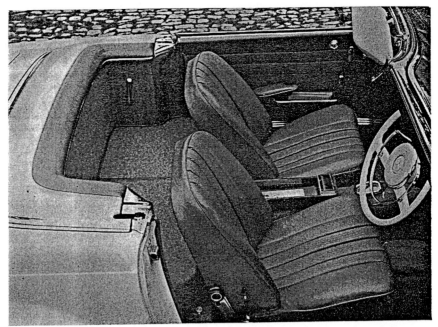

Deep, well-upholstered seats are getting on for perfection, and the arm-rests are exactly right. Behind the seats is room for an (optional) sideways passenger seat

ever be overturned. Right through the speed range the car feels most stable whatever the road surface is like, and at higher speeds it loses all traces of harshness and is notably pitch- and roll-free.

The brakes are light and progressive, pulling the car up very surely from high speed, but there was some roughness from the front discs which might have been the result of some imbalance; it was not noticed at low speed when the 230SL could be stopped with very light pedal pressure. Lighting too is quite excellent, proving adequate all the way up to 120 mph although the dipped beam, with its sharp Continental cut-off, is not good for much more than half this speed.

That the Mercedes averaged a fraction better than 20 mpg throughout the test is particularly deserving of note, for this is not a light car and the engine is working hard; also, of course, the automatic transmission is likely to make the car use a little more fuel and a long motorway trip did not improve the consumption. Probably an owner could get near 25 mpg on a long and not too rapid journey,

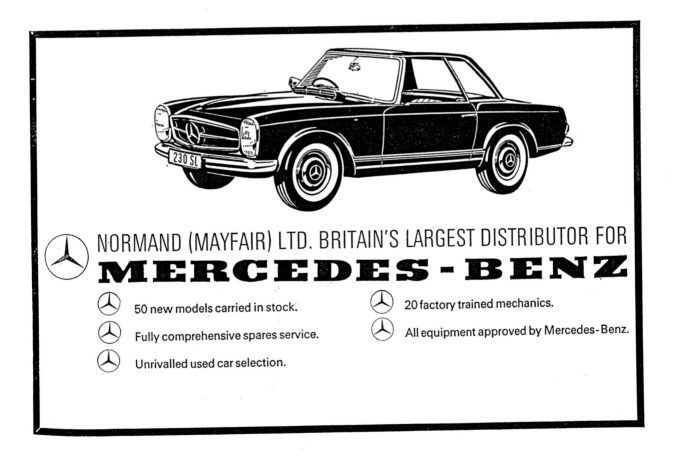

for we know that the petrol injection system is inherently economical.

Comfort first

When the hardtop is fitted the 230SL is as quiet, comfortable and draught-free as any good saloon, and we noticed that the heavy " lid " is beautifully trimmed. Four levers only have to be moved to release the top in a matter of seconds, but it is too heavy for one person to lift off and even when two people do the job, care has to be taken not to scratch the body paint. In a movable sill behind the seats the hood is furled, so the car can be fixed-head, open, or closed in about one minute flat!

The furniture is, of course, *par excellence*. Seating, always the most important feature, is perhaps the best we have tried. The cushions, covered by a synthetic material, are quite firm but carefully shaped to hold the occupants secure when the car is cornered fast, and the range of seat and backrest adjustment is sufficient to keep everyone happy. There are one or two jarring notes in such a nice living room. The white steering wheel is thick-rimmed and heavy looking, and we would much prefer a nice wood-rim wheel. The handbrake is much too far away as this has not been converted from left-hand drive, and for

SPECIFICATION
MERCEDES-BENZ 230SL

ENGINE:

Six cylinders; bore 82 mm (3.23 in); stroke 72.8 mm (2.87 in). Cubic capacity 2,306 cc. Compression ratio 9.3 to 1. Maximum bhp (net) 150 at 5,500 rpm: maximum torque 144 lb ft at 4,500 rpm. Bosch fuel injection with 6-plunger Bosch electric pump. Chain-driven ohc valves. Tank capacity 14.3 gallons, water capacity 20 pints, sump capacity 9.7 pints. 12v 52 amp/hr battery.

TRANSMISSION:

Daimler Benz fluid coupling with 4-speed epicyclic gearbox. Overall gear ratios: 1st, 3.98; 2nd, 2.52; 3rd, 1.58; 4th, 1.1. Gearing, 19.7 mph per 1,000 rpm in top gear.

CHASSIS:

Suspension, front: independent by coils and wishbones, augmented by rubber springs. Rear, independent by low-pivot swing axles with coil springs, radius arms and horizontal compensating spring. Bilstein telescopic shock absorbers front and rear. Brakes, 9.9 in discs front, 9.1 in drums rear with twin circuits and servo assistance. DB recirculating ball steering with power assistance. Pressed steel disc wheels. Firestone Phoenix tyres, 185-14 radial ply.

DIMENSIONS:

	ft	in
Wheelbase	7	10.5
Track, front	4	10
Track, rear	4	9.75
Overall length	14	1.75
Overall width	5	9
Overall height	4	4
Ground clearance		6.75
Turning circle	30	7
Kerb weight	25.5 cwt	

PERFORMANCE:

mph	
0 - 30	4.3
0 - 40	5.8
0 - 50	7.8
0 - 60	10.6
0 - 70	14.0
0 - 80	18.4
0 - 90	25.5
0 - 100	34.2

MAXIMUM SPEED IN GEARS:

	mph
1st	28
2nd	50
3rd	80
4th	117

Overall fuel consumption: 21.2 mpg

PRICE: With automatic transmission £3,865 16 3
Power steering   93 0 10

£3,958 17 1

preference we should like the fascia to be leather covered rather than painted. Finally, the light switch is awkwardly placed behind the steering wheel.

Unusual for a Continental car, there is carpet on the floor with sensible rubber mats where the wear takes place. The area behind the seats, intended for a dog, suitcase, or semi-prostrate and uncomfortable passenger, has a whip-cord carpet.

Big instruments face the driver through the large (17in) wheel, consisting of a 140 mph speedometer and a 7000 rpm tachometer with red blob at 6500. In a vertical panel are the fuel, oil pressure and water temperature gauges, plus all the usual warning lights. A neat "do-everything" lever from the right of the column works the indicators, flashes the lights, stops and starts the screen-wipers, and operates the screenwashers (which didn't work on the test car). An inset button speeds the wipers up.

Heater controls are rather complicated, but the system is effective once mastered. Hot or cold air can be blown through the fascia vents, and there are butterfly nozzles to keep the side windows clear. Other items which appear in the specification are a cigar lighter, dipping mirror, electric clock, a map light in the locker lid, and a carrier for oddments on the transmission tunnel.

We parted with the 230SL with rather mixed feelings—

The large and 'heavy' steering wheel may not be to everyone's taste. Instruments are clear, ventilation comprehensive, but handbrake and light switch (below tachometer) are awkwardly placed

and the wish to try a manual gearbox car for comparison. Like a well-bred woman, the car is so nice that it can be quite boring at times, and it could be even better if it had the extra character that better performance—or a few vices —would impart. But as a touring car it has few equals.

287 : 1966 Mercedes-Benz 230SL

PERFORMANCE CHECK

(Figures in brackets are those of the original Road Test, published 2 October 1964).

0 to 30 mph.	**4.3** sec (4.6)	In top gear:		
0 to 40 mph	**5.9** sec (6.1)			
0 to 50 mph	**8.1** sec (8.4)	30 to 50 mph	**12.3** sec (11.7)	
0 to 60 mph	**10.9** sec (11.4)	40 to 60 mph	**12.1** sec (12.1)	
0 to 70 mph	**14.6** sec (15.1)	50 to 70 mph	**12.8** sec (13.2)	
0 to 80 mph	**19.3** sec (20.0)	60 to 80 mph	**15.4** sec (14.3)	
0 to 90 mph	**28.0** sec (26.9)	70 to 90 mph	**17.2** sec (16.1)	
0 to 100 mph	**40.7** sec (34.9)	80 to 100 mph	**21.4** sec (17.9)	
Standing ¼ mile	**18.3** sec (18.1)	Standing Km	**33.6** sec (—)	

PRICES

Car for sale at Reading at	£3,1
Typical trade advertised price for same age and model in average condition	£3,0
Total cost of car when new including tax	£3,8
Depreciation over 2¾ years	£7
Annual depreciation as proportion of cost new	6¾ per ce

DATA

Date first registered	17 February 19(
Number of owners	
Tax expires	31 December 19(
M.O.T.	Not yet d
Fuel consumption	18-20 m(
Oil consumption	200 m(
Mileometer reading	27,9(

TYRES

Size: 185-HR-14in. Firestone Phoenix radials. Appr(cost per replacement cover £12 18s 9d. Depth original tread 9mm; remaining tread depth. 5m(front, 8mm rear, 2mm on spare.

TOOLS

Original kit complete and little used. No handbo(with car.

CAR FOR SALE AT:

Vincents of Reading Ltd., Station Square, Readin(Berkshire. Telephone: Reading 54204.

WHENEVER the occasional Mercedes-Benz is included in this series, it invariably confirms the Stuttgart legend of longevity; naturally one does not expect much to be wrong with a quality car less than three years old, but it is really delightful to find almost total absence of any deterioration. This 230SL could almost have come from Mercedes press officer Eric Johnson at Brentford as our long-awaited 280SL for full Autotest, and not until we had found the 2,306 c.c. engine under the bonnet instead of the latest 2,778 unit, and spotted a D year letter and 28,000 miles on the speedometer, would we have noticed the difference. It is in every way up to scratch mechanically, exactly like the one we tested as a new car (and in the same colour incidentally) just over four years ago.

Starting is always slow with this fuel injection, but there is no cold starting control to bother with and the engine always fires after a short run on the starter. Slight differences of injector settings may have accounted for the fact that this 230SL proved a little faster up to 80 mph, but slower at higher speeds, taking about 6 sec longer to reach 100 mph. The engine is still in peak condition and returns the same fuel consumption of about 18 mpg, and only slightly heavier oil consumption, as did the original car.

Automatic transmission is fitted, and because of the control allowed over the three upper gears by means of a central stick selector, it makes the car, in most opinions, even more enjoyable to drive than the manual gearbox model. The transmission is particularly responsive to throttle opening, and is designed to get the best out of the engine. It needs little prompting to change down, and if a fairly wide throttle opening suggests that you really mean business for

overtaking, it holds second or third right up to 6,000 rpm.

In hard driving there is a lot of engine noise, reminding the driver that taxation laws in Germany demand relatively small, rather hard-worked engines, but in moderate driving the engine seemed less fussy than in the original Road Test car. A Kenlowe fan replaces the positively driven standard fan, and this obviously accounts for much of the noise reduction. The fan cuts in unobtrusively after a minute or two when the car is stuck in traffic, and can be heard if a window is opened. There is also an over-riding switch but we found no use for it.

Power steering is fitted, but the driver can be excused for not knowing until he sees the extra drive belt under the bonnet. The steering still retains its beautiful precision, quick response and good self-centring; and it is light but not at all woolly. One has to know the unassisted control to appreciate how much effort is saved. The car can be cornered really fast and with great confidence; with its wide track, all-independent suspension (swing axles with low pivot, at rear), and low build, the 230SL sits down very well indeed on fast corners. At speed on the straight directional stability is good unless it is windy, when there is quite a lot of reaction through the steering as the car gets buffeted about. It is suspected that wheel balance needs attention; vibration begins to be noticed at about 75 mph, and continues right through to 90 before the car runs smoothly again.

Unlike the 280SL, which has discs all round, the rear brakes of the 230SL are drums; but response to the pedal is very good indeed and there is terrific servo assistance. With fierce braking there is perhaps a little too much nose dive, but this is characteristic, and the chief weakness of an otherwise excellent suspension.

It gives a particularly soft ride, without any floa(or plunge. Familiar sections of neglected road ar(ironed out so well by the 230SL that they migh(almost have been resurfaced. The handbrake i(on the passenger side of the transmission tunnel—quite a long reach, especially whe(wearing safety belts, but it is very effective; ther(is also a positive transmission lock in Park

Even £1,500 is a great sum of money to pa(for a used car, opening the price range to man(fine and luxurious models, and when it come(to more than twice this amount, £3,150 seem(an appalling sum to pay for a car nearly thre(years old. However, we have no doubt that i(will sell at this figure, and it should give long lasting pleasure and satisfaction to whoeve(buys it.

CONDITION SUMMARY
Bodywork

As first seen in the attractively laid-out show-room at Reading, the appearance of this Mercedes was indistinguishable from that of a brand new car, but when we were able to examine it more carefully under natural light a few tell-tale signs could be spotted to show that the paintwork is not all original. There has been some local respray work, but it has been executed to highest standard, no doubt by the UK Conces-sionaires themselves. The paintwork is in "midnight" blue, which admirably suits the attractive lines of the 230SL. A small touched-in blemish above the nearside front wheel arch is the only flaw on otherwise perfect finish. All the chromium and stainless steel brightwork is to equally high standard, marred only by a few kerb scratches on one of the wheel trims. The car

Although very expensively priced this car is in such beautiful condition that it represents quite attractive used-car value. The interior is almost as new, and the engine compartment is clean

must have been very well cared for to have such impeccable interior condition. Even the seats show little creasing but there are some chafe marks, perhaps from suitcases carried on the back shelf, behind the seats. The underneath is protected by thorough undersealing, and completely free from rust. Visible deterioration throughout the car is negligible.

Equipment

This is the Coupé-Convertible model, with neat and easily detachable hardtop in position; the rear "tonneau cover" panel lifts to reveal a very substantial and again easily fitted hood for summer use. Every item of the standard equipment and added extras is in perfect working order, including fog and parking lamps, and the comprehensive instrumentation. The speedometer is within 2 mph at 100 mph.

Accessories

A push button Motorola radio is fitted, coupled to an aerial with electric remote control. Be-neath the radio is a little unit with two numbered dials—the burglar alarm. Unless the correct combination is set, the horn sounds when the ignition key is turned. Such an accessory seems superfluous on a car already fitted as standard with a steering column lock. Other accessories are Britax seat belts and the Kenlowe fan.

About the 230SL

First introduction of the 230SL was in 1963 for the Geneva Show, as replacement for the four-cylinder 1,897 c.c. 190SL. The chassis was based on that of the 220S and SE saloons, with all-independent suspension using low-pivot swing axles at the rear. Standard transmission was four-speed all-synchromesh, but Daimler-Benz automatic was available "upon special request"; later, of course, it developed into a listed and very popular option. The six-cylinder power unit was similar to that of the 220SE, but with bore increased by 2mm, giving bore and stroke of 82 x 72.8 mm, and capacity 2,306 c.c. With 9.3 to 1 compression (instead of 8.7 in the saloons), and fuel injection as standard, net power was 150 bhp at 5,600 rpm. Power steering was an unusual option for a sports car, and the 230SL also introduced the multiple finger-tip control unit for washers, wipers, indicators and dipping and flashing headlamps, which has gradually spread throughout the Mercedes range.

In this form, production ran for four years, until the 1967 Geneva Show, when the new seven-main-bearing 250 engine (2,496 c.c.) was fitted, giving considerably more torque but, surprisingly, no increase in peak power. Buyers of the 250SL must have been disappointed to find it out-dated in less than a year by introduction of the 280SL in January this year. It continued the original 230SL body style with remarkably few changes, but was now powered by the 2,778 c.c. engine. Power output increased to 170 bhp net at 5,600 rpm, disc brakes were fitted all round in place of the previous disc front, drum rear system, but it retained the swing axle rear suspension. □

Meet Mercedes (230 SL).
She has designs on men with money.

Men of whatever age or means might do well to stay out of flirting range of the Mercedes 230 SL.

Lest they become involved.

For this classy, sporty young one knows an uncanny lot about men and what it takes to make them fall in love with a fine motorcar.

Regard some of her charms that could very well turn the heads of the most respectable members of your community:

She was born and bred on the most wicked race courses in the world.

And brought to sophisticated refinement on the speed-limitless Autobahn and the boulevards of the world's most renowned capitals.

The 230 SL is a two-seater roadster. And so much more !

It is a Grand Touring Car with all the classic features called for in that strict and high level classification.

It is fully instrumented. You get very fast, excellent synchromesh through the manual gear box. Or sporty-acting automatic transmission, if you want.

Its loving heart of a fuel injection engine will beat all day at 125 m.p.h.

This temptress is now displaying her charms at your Mercedes-Benz dealer's. One look might not hurt.

Be brazen. Take the wife along.

MERCEDES-BENZ

30

230SL appetizer

SINCE our references to the 230SL Mercedes at the Total foreign car test day last year, many readers have requested that we conduct a full scale road test. It was our intentions that such a test should appear in this issue, but unfortunately the road test car, which was being brought from Germany, did not arrive in time to allow us to conduct a full scale test. We did, however, manage to have an afternoon's driving of a 230SL, on roads in and around London, and since this is a vastly different proposition to a high speed dash around the Silverstone circuit our impressions are perhaps worth recording here, even though the full road test of the car should not be too long away.

There are three models of the 230SL in theory, although in practice they are merely equipment variations. The car we drove had a folding hood and a detachable hardtop, but the model is also provided with detachable hardtop and without folding hood or with folding hood and no detachable hardtop. It was also equipped with power steering, power brakes and automatic transmission. A very understandable reaction to this would be to say 'and they call it a sports car'. Truth to tell, there is very little of the traditional sports car about the 230SL. It is luxuriously, almost opulently equipped; the springing is soft; the controls are light; the engine is not noisy and, on this version at least, there is no need to change gear at all if you do not wish. In short, it might appear to be a thoroughly pansy motor car.

But this is only telling part of the story. Who wants noise, smell and disc-slipping suspension if the element of enjoyment inherent in a sports car, which is its whole *raison d'etre* if you like, can still be had without them. This is the case with the 230SL. One very quickly becomes accustomed to and appreciative of the very small physical effort that goes into driving the car, but this enhances rather than detracts from the feeling of control that results. With its finger-light touch, the steering is precise. The lightness of the brakes encourages delicacy in the retarding process, while as for the automatic transmission—anathema and horror to the true-blue sports car fan—not only does it provide complete relaxation in the inevitably congested city driving that we have to put up with these days, it also offers positive control of ratios with no loss other than exercise to the left leg. Handily mounted in the central position that is almost obligatory with a sports car, the transmission control lever is well placed for changes up and down. Third and top are instantaneously engaged by a half-inch movement backward or forward and a gate intervenes to prevent inadvertent engagement of second gear. The positions are, of course, not for a single ratio but merely 'hold' devices which prevent the engagement of a higher gear while selected. In our short drive, we were quickly getting a great deal of fun out of the use of this transmission.

Driving position, instruments and minor controls are all first class, the seats being really substantial affairs with adjustable backrests and a large range of fore and aft movement. There are winding windows, a central oddments tray and a glove locker. Rev counter and speedometer are mounted directly in front of the driver with supplementary instruments in between. Fresh air ventilation is provided through two adjustable vents at either side of the dash, and an efficient heater will either heat outside air or recirculate interior air. Behind the seats there is space for luggage or for small children. There are winding windows and a neat metal cover conceals the soft top as shown below, while the hardtop makes the interior indistinguishable from a saloon. Luggage space is good and all round visibility excellent. A slightly incongruous note is struck inside by the use of woodwork in one or two rather unexpected places.

On the handling side, we had little opportunity to exploit the potential of the car in the small time at our disposal. The leech-like road holding which the car evinced at Silverstone was certainly apparent in the few occasions that we were able to take a corner at any speed at all. For a fuller assessment we look forward to the road test that we expect to be able to conduct before long.

MERCEDES 230SL

—The now well-known and highly-reputed Mercedes 230SL sports car was introduced to replace the Model 190SL. Design is based generally on the medium-class series of the marque, but with differences in frame, floor assembly and bodywork as necessitated by its being in the sporting idiom. Several chassis sub-assemblies including front axle, steering gear, transmission, drive shaft, rear axle and brakes are similar to those used in the 220SB/SEB. Overall dimensions are the same as those of the 190SL.

BODYWORK

The frame-floor assembly is of new design and incorporates the familiar principle of combining resilient front and rear sections with a stiff, robust mid-section. Because the roof cannot be used as a supporting element, the design called for a particularly robust frame-floor, and the box-type propeller shaft tunnel materially assists this aim of rigidity.

The detachable top section is an innovation, and incorporates two additional side windows as compared with the previous model. Despite its light appearance, the structure is very strong. A folding hood, stored in a recess between passenger and luggage compartments, can be fitted if the car is used as an open roadster.

The 230SL has two independent front seats and, as an optional extra, a rear emergency seat mounted at 90° to the fore-and-aft axis. Backrest adjustment by handwheel is a feature and the squabs are secured against forward tipping by a device

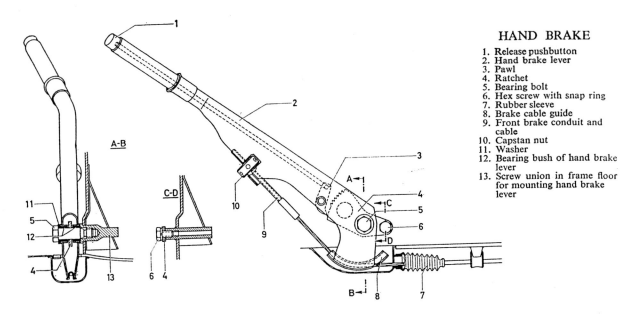

HAND BRAKE

1. Release pushbutton
2. Hand brake lever
3. Pawl
4. Ratchet
5. Bearing bolt
6. Hex screw with snap ring
7. Rubber sleeve
8. Brake cable guide
9. Front brake conduit and cable
10. Capstan nut
11. Washer
12. Bearing bush of hand brake lever
13. Screw union in frame floor for mounting hand brake lever

operated from either side. Arrangement of instrumentation and lighting are as on the 220SEB cabriolet. The heating system includes a two-stage blower.

Air ducts for ventilation during warm weather are provided at each side of the facia.

BRAKES

The system is the same as that used on the 220SEB. The front brakes are of Girling disc type, whilst the rears are of normal drum type with Alfin drums. Disc and drum brakes operate on separate hydraulic circuits, both of which are controlled by a tandem master cylinder. The brake energiser, type T 51/200 is vacuum-operated, and acts directly on the piston of the master cylinder.

CLUTCH

The 230SL is equipped with the same type of clutch as is fitted to the 2·2-litre Mercedes range.

ELECTRICAL SYSTEM

A three-phase generator provides power at idling as well as higher speeds.

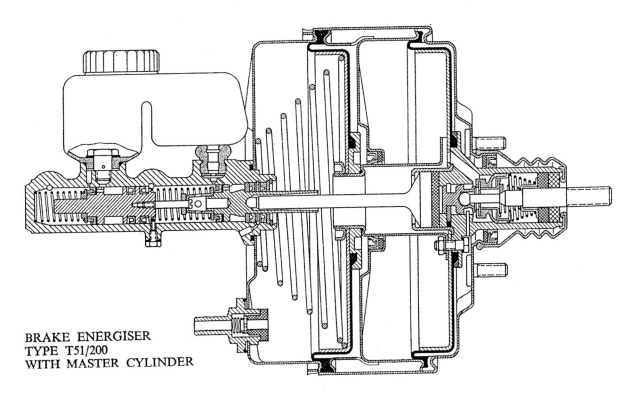

BRAKE ENERGISER
TYPE T51/200
WITH MASTER CYLINDER

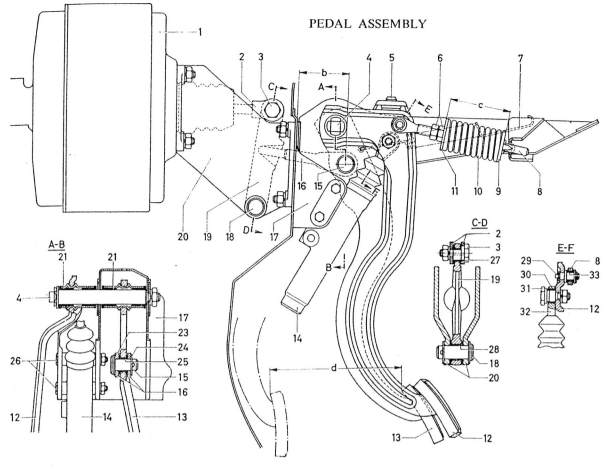

1. Brake energiser type T 51/200
2. Piston rod of brake energiser
3. Adjusting screw with snap ring and hex nut
4. Bearing bolt
5. Rubber stop for clutch pedal
6. Hex nut
7. Release spring for brake pedal
8. Push rod
9. Spring seat
10. Compression spring
11. Spring seat
12. Clutch pedal
13. Brake pedal
14. Hydraulic cylinder
15. Capstan screw
16. Push rod
17. Pedal assembly support
18. Capstan screw
19. Intermediate lever
20. Bearing support
21. Bearing bush
23. Washer
24. Spring washer
25. Bearing bush
26. Hex screw with snap ring and hex nut
27. Bearing bush
28. Bearing bush
29. Bearing bolt
30. Bearing bush
31. Adjusting screw with snap ring and hex nut
32. Piston rod of hydraulic cylinder
33. Bearing bush

ENGINE

GENERAL.—The 6-cylinder power unit is a modified version of the type used in the 220SEB. Notable features are increased displacement, six-plunger fuel injection and modified design of fuel inlet and camshaft. The engine develops 150 h.p. (DIN) at 5,500 r.p.m., maximum torque being 20 mkg. (DIN) at 4,200 r.p.m. and maximum engine speed 6,500 r.p.m. The cylinder bore is 82 mm. as compared with the 80 mm. of the 220SE.

CAMSHAFT.—Design no longer includes the annular grooves provided on the second, third and fourth pivot. Instead, each camshaft bearing is equipped with an oil groove and oil pocket. As on the 2·2-litre units, the bearings and cams are lubricated by gravity feed from an outside oil pipe. The camshaft of the 230SL can be identified by the number 76 punched in the front end.

CYLINDER HEAD.—To accommodate the injection nozzles protruding into each of the six fuel-intake ducts, the upper valve-gear housing has been correspondingly recessed. As compared with the 2·2-litre units, the size of the compression chambers was reduced, resulting in a compression ratio of 9·3:1. Valves are fitted with rotating caps fitted to the cylinder head in recessed mountings. Design of valve guides, which are shorter than those of the 2·2-litre units, is suited to the valve-stem sealing system which comprises a Teflon sealing ring, a locking ring and a securing strap. Except for diameters, design is the same for inlet and exhaust valves. The design of the combustion chambers also called for a new type of head gasket.

CONNECTING RODS.—Diameter of bores in connecting rods is 51·6 mm. (54 mm. in 2·2-litre units). The bores are fitted with thin-walled bearing bushes. This design feature ensures greater stiffness of the rods and enables them to withstand the increased loads resulting from the higher engine revolutions.

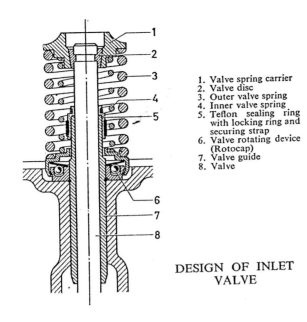

1. Valve spring carrier
2. Valve disc
3. Outer valve spring
4. Inner valve spring
5. Teflon sealing ring with locking ring and securing strap
6. Valve rotating device (Rotocap)
7. Valve guide
8. Valve

DESIGN OF INLET VALVE

PISTONS.—The increase in cylinder diameter necessitated the use of larger pistons having a diameter of 82 mm. Pistons are fitted with four compression rings and a slotted flat oil ring with expansion spring. Whereas gudgeon pins are 3 mm. longer than those in the 2·2-litre types, their diameter has remained unchanged.

FRONT END AND FRONT SUSPENSION

The front axle and its suspension correspond with the design used in types 220SEB coupe and cabriolet.

FUEL INJECTION SYSTEM

The system differs from that of the 220SEB. Although the principle of intermittent fuel injection was retained, the nozzles no longer discharge into the suction pipe, but into the fuel inlet duct arranged in the cylinder head, which is heated by the cooling water.

Unlike the 220SEB, the 230SL has a fuel injection pump with six pump elements. The injection nozzles discharging into the inlet ducts interconnect with the pump elements by injection lines. During fuel injection, which is timed to coincide with the suction stroke, a portion of the fuel is injected through the open valve into the combustion chamber. The atomised fuel absorbs heat from its surroundings and thus provides additional interior cooling of the cylinders.

The solenoid-operated starter valve is not at the end of the suction pipe as on the 220SEB but is centrally arranged on the pipe so that the fuel jets are directed towards the individual fuel inlet ducts.

The idle-air duct is designed as a separate pipe above the inlet ducts, with which it interconnects by ports. Idle air is taken from the space between the air filter and the valve socket. The throttle screw is arranged directly in front of the idle-air duct.

Apart from the six pump-elements, the injection system incorporated in the 230 differs from that of the 2·2-litre models in the design of the governor, which does not operate with cam disc and lever, but with a cam scanned by a roller so that the governing rod suits operating conditions. Cam motion is controlled by the centrifugal governor (dependent on engine speed) and by a linkage connected to the governor linkage (dependent on load conditions). No essential changes were made in the arrangement of the governing lever of the injection pump and the throttle valve.

GEARBOX

The general system is similar to that used on the 2·2-litre cars, with floor-mounted lever. An optional extra is the DB automatic gearbox with gear selector lever arranged as a neat floor-mounted stick and gate.

REAR AXLE

Reduction ratio of the rear axle is 3·75:1. As in the case of the 220SEB coupe and cabriolet, the rear axle is seated in barrel roller bearings.

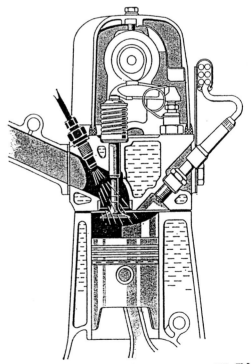

LOCATION OF INJECTION NOZZLE IN CYLINDER HEAD

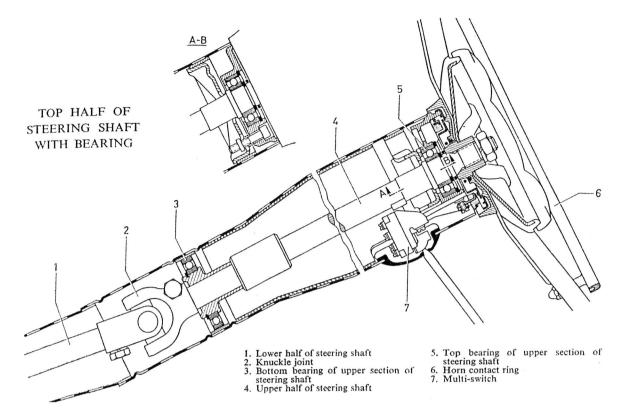

TOP HALF OF
STEERING SHAFT
WITH BEARING

1. Lower half of steering shaft
2. Knuckle joint
3. Bottom bearing of upper section of steering shaft
4. Upper half of steering shaft
5. Top bearing of upper section of steering shaft
6. Horn contact ring
7. Multi-switch

SUSPENSION AND SHOCK ABSORBERS

Basically, the suspension and damping are as used throughout the steel-sprung medium class range. The individual springs, as well as the torsion bar stabiliser on the front axle, are of slightly different design. Shock absorbers are the type used on the 220SEB. Front suspension characteristics are very much the same as those of the 220SEB coupe and cabriolet but the torsion bar has a 'harder' effect. Rear springs are harder, and the compensating springs softer than the types fitted to the 2·2-litre models.

STEERING

The mechanical steering gear used on the Mercedes medium class range has also been used on the 230SL, but by suitably angling the steering column, which is fitted with a universal joint, the best position for the sporting configuration is obtained.

The upper section of the steering column inner shaft, which is relatively short, runs in ball-bearings at each end, and the bottom bearing is of large diameter. The knuckle-type universal joint is immediately below the bottom bearing.

WHEELS AND TYRES

The car is fitted with 14 in. wheels and radial-ply tyres. Method of wheel mounting and adjustment is different, since instead of being fastened by ball collar studs and centred by ball collar nuts screwed on to the hub studs, the wheels of the 230SL are accommodated in a central bore with a certain degree of tolerance, and held by ball collar studs.

for the perfectionist

230 SL

NORMAND (MAYFAIR) LTD.
have the perfect car

Prove it to your own demanding standards. Drive one of Europe's most sought-after cars and discover what the words comfort, luxury and performance can mean in terms of Mercedes motoring.

We'll be delighted to lay on a test drive at any time you like—and pick you up from your front door too. All you have to do is telephone and name the model. They are all outstanding. All share in the Mercedes reputation for perfect motoring. And in two cases the price is less than £2,000!

Showroom: Avenfield House,
127 Park Lane, London W.I.

MAY 5831

Service and Spares: Cumberland
Garage, Bryanston Street,
London W.I.

GRO 8801

 MERCEDES-BENZ

Mercedes-Benz 230-280

FOR the first Mercedes-Benz car to be covered in our Classic Choice series, we have chosen the very popular "Pagoda Roof" 230, 250 and 280SL sports coupés. These are not as scarce as the earlier 300SL's nor as valuable (especially in the case of the "Gullwings")\nor are they as thirsty as the model which succeeded them. Thus they can make excellent choices for the Mercedes fancier, even if they are no longer in the bargain basement for price. What *is* clear, though, is that there is no shortage of people wanting one and many exchange earlier, high mileage examples for later, low mileage examples rather than buy something else altogether. Which is a first class recommendation for the breed.

Of course these later cars lacked some of the outright sportiness of the legendary 300SL, and some enthusiasts were, understandably, disappointed by the new car. But for space, comfort and roadholding the later car was a definite improvement, while its classically simple but elegant looks were instantly appealing. That this Mercedes-Benz coupé has stood the test of time so well that its styling is as fresh and clean today, nearly twenty years after it was first shown, is a remarkable testimony to good design. The 230SL was first shown at the 1963 Geneva Show and it used chassis components similar to those of the 220S and SE saloons of the period. The rear track of 4ft 10.5in was identical but the wheelbase, naturally, was shorter at 7ft 10 in. The same front double wishbone suspension was used, with the single-joint low-pivot swing axles for the independent rear end common to Daimler-Benz products at that time. The wheel size went up an inch to 14in, which in conjunction with a higher axle ratio gave more relaxed cruising with a 19.6mph per 1000rpm final gearing.

The 230SL's 2,306cc engine was obtained by increasing the bore of the 220 by 2mm. A six plunger fuel injection pump fed nozzles in the cylinder head ports and the compression ratio was increased to 9.3 to 1 high for the time. Although 170bhp was quoted, its true output was probably more like 150bhp. Otherwise, this six cylinder unit has overhead valves operated by a single chain-driven overhead camshaft via bucket tappets, but at this time the crankshaft was carried by only four main bearings.

Although a manual gearbox was available, many in this country had a Daimler-Benz four speed automatic gearbox with fluid coupling — although the later, improved torque converter gearboxes came with the 280 saloons, this was never fitted to the SL's in this series which finally died in February 1971. So too, though a rather heavy and low geared manual steering was available, the optional extra power steering was generally preferred making it, probably, the first sports car to be so equipped. Clearly one of the model's most delightful attributes is its adaptability. Originally the 230S1 was offered as a roadster (i.e. open), or a closed coupé but most in Great Britain came with the most desirable option of the three, a hood *and* a removable hardtop. Thus, during the summer months, the owner could enjoy fresh air, with the hood available as protection from showers, but in the winter fit the hardtop which had the added advantages of improving visibility and enhancing the lines of the car generally.

If the body was to remain essentially the same throughout the life of the model, the engine *was* subject to revision. Four years after the initial

The 230SL. This example has automatic transmission and the cost, when new, wa £3,667.

launch, and again at Geneva, the 250SL took a bow. A new cylinder engine with seven main bearings for greater refinement was the order of the day and the stroke increased from 72.8mm to 78.8mm bringing the capacity up to 2,496cc. Other changes saw the rear drum brakes of the 230SL's replaced by disc on the 250, while vestigal rear seats were fitted on the coupé model. Barely nine months after this, the engine was bored-out to 86.5mm to create the 280SL. This was an altogether better unit with no startling increase in power, but its greatly improved torque made the car more flexible and easier and more restful to drive — however this would have been small comfort to someone who had just taken delivery of the 250SL.

Even a motor car as superbly engineered as a Mercedes-Benz cannot be expected to be faultless, and when upwards of ten years have elapsed it would be living in cloud-cuckoo land not to make some allowances for age in a piece of machinery.

It should also be said at this point that the SL's were expensive playthings when new, so if you fancy yourself as a playboy, or playgirl for that matter, you must be prepared to treat the car in the manner to which it should have been accustomed. That means, inevitably, that servicing and parts will be greater than for a Morris Minor, but they are nowhere near as horrific as popular legend would have you believe. The main advantages, though, are that the car is made to last, made to be used hard, and when you do need parts, even body panels, they are available from the factory. And that really is a plus point.

To find out about the faults and failings, I went along to experts Woking Motors of Hersham, Surrey, who are the oldest Mercedes-Benz distributors in the country.

Bodywork and chassis

Such is the truly excellent build quality of the SL's, and indeed all Mercedes-Benz products, that corrosion problems are minimal on any but the most poorly cared-for and abused examples. Those who read these pages regularly will know that this is a rare statement for us to be able to make on a post-war car, barring those with glass-fibre bodies. As well as the metal of the basic shell, the paintwork and bright metal is also

A 230 engine, with fuel injection pipes, in evidence.

of above average standard with very good last qualities. Indeed, the casual observer can be v shocked to learn the age of one of these vehic especially if it is carrying a personalised num plate. Which is why so many still prefer to one; it cuts more of a dash at the Golf Club t any new Granada could for the same price.

If they must rust, and some do, the places to watch are along the seam on the top of the front wing, its inner panel, the sills (inevitably) and the corners of the boot floor if the rubber seals have been letting water through. On poor examples the box section just behind the radiator can rust and, more seriously, the chassis by the rear axle mountings. Of course some potential buyers, might be quite prepared to take on a poor example at a lower price and carry out a full-scale restoration, but those not wishing to do this and opting to pay the full price will be well advised to take with them a magnet. Alas the high prices and desirability of the model brings out the worst in some people, and some good looking SL's may just be full of skillfully applied "bodge". So beware lest you pay over the odds for a full-scale rebuild that you had not bargained for.

Given that you find yourself in that unfortunate position or you suffer crash damage during ownership, it is most reassuring to know that body panels are available. The front wings, for example, are a reasonable £63 or thereabouts, and sills £20. The danger zone, as far as the bank manager is concerned, being the front lamp units: each lamp assembly is £85, with another £28 for the surround and a further £8.65 for the headlamp bowl. Fortunately these lamps, variously Bosch or Hella, have a life of 40-50,000 miles but if you are planning an accident try to avoid smashing them!

One thing that is becoming scarce as well as expensive is the chrome trim, but there's nothing to stop you having it re-chromed by one of the many specialists. Also the strip of wood veneer on the fascia, particularly in open cars, may deteriorate with age but can be refurbished by the amateur quite successfully. The hood, naturally, should be checked for tears and for proper operation and the hardtop for a good fit and A1 condition seals, otherwise leaks and wind noise will result.

Engine, gearbox and back axle

The engine is designed for a long life and plenty of hard use, and bore life is in the 80-100,000 mile region, though Woking Motors have seen examples go well beyond that figure. The four bearing crank 230's and 250's, though, may need a regrind and new bearings before bore wear reaches the embarrassing stage. The oil pressure gauge is slightly pointless as the needle shoots up to the maximum 45psi reading upon starting up the engine and there it should stay at all normal running speeds. Suspect anything less even when warm at above 1,500rpm.

Unfortunately this model tends to be a second car or used for short journeys, which can do more harm than good and lead to a more rapid bore wear than is correct. A good "thrash" every now and then is said to do wonders! However when the dreaded day comes that an overhaul of part or all of the engine is necessary, then the bills will come home to roost. A top overhaul with new valves, freshly cut seats, and the cylinder head skimmed will come to about £300. A set of new pistons will set you back about the same amount, while if you are unlucky enough to require a short block, don't expect much change from £900. On the other hand a short engine saves the garage time, and time as we know, means money — and, of course, it's guaranteed.

Fortunately the fuel injection pump has a very long life, about the only problem being that the pump rack can stick causing over-rich running. The unit can be overhauled if there are any problems, so don't let anyone try to tell you it cannot just so that they can present you with a £700 bill for a new pump.

As with the engine the gearbox is a reliable unit in automatic form. It has four speeds and is of the fluid-coupling type — the torque converter gearbox was never fitted to this model in the UK. It must be said that the gearchanges were never the smoothest around but there should not be any shocks transmitted. Naturally a check should be made for leaks, and a good test for whether the 'box may need an overhaul is to remove the dipstick and smell it. Yes really! There will be a quite distinctive smell of burning in the oil if the news is bad.

Of the rarer manual boxes there are both four and ZF five speed versions, with the latter being the most desirable for long-legged cruising. However parts for it are more difficult to obtain and pricey, when you can get them.

There are rarely, if ever, problems with the back axle which is extremely robust. Just watch for excessive leakage.

Suspension, steering and brakes

The front suspension is generally trouble-free, but problems can arise from faulty servicing, especially if this has not been carried out by an approved agent. Often missed are the two grease nipples on the top wishbones. If the top knuckles have been starved of grease they will usually squeak when the front of the car is pressed down or the car goes over a bump. In bad cases a whole wishbone assembly may be needed. The bottom knuckles can seize too, but are easier to deal with. The trackrod ends are not adjustable. Kingpins and bottom bushes can be checked with a jack under the wishbone to take the weight off the car. Examples on prices: kingpins per side are £35; bottom bushes £15 and top swivel kit £10.

At the back end, two bushes on the swing axles can wear and make for strange handling through rear steer effect — the tyre lever check is really the only way if you are not sure. Front back suspension is aided by telescopic gas-filled shock absorbers manufactured by Bilstein or Fischel & Sachs and should be watched for excessive leaks (they all weep a bit) and changed when no longer functioning properly. There are a number of proprietary makes of shock absorber around too that may be fitted with equal satisfaction.

On the steering is a damper — like a small shock absorber — which should be checked for leaks and efficiency. Failure here will transmit an unacceptable amount of road shock through to the steering wheel. The steering box and pump have a very long life being permanently lubricated — just watch for leaks again.

The brakes on the 230 have adjustable rear shoes, but the 250 and 280 models have an all-disc system. Pads are £10-£14 per set and if you score the discs badly, they're £34 each. The hydraulics are tandem operated, and Mercedes-Benz recommend annual renewal of fluid for maximum efficiency.

Sum up, prices, clubs

The best recommendation for a car of this marque is its service history. Really good, clean, one owner cars are sought after but they certainly exist. Prices can range from £3,000 up to £5,000 for an average to good example and £8,000 or more for a concours example.

You can do no better than belong to the Mercedes-Benz Club whose Secretary is Biddy Gupwell, of The Firs, Biscombe, Churchstanton, Taunton, Somerset. (Tel: 082 360 385)

Last but not least I would like to thank the helpful and enthusiastic Woking Motors of Hersham, Surrey, led by Director Owen Williams, and his Service Manager and staff for their help in compiling this article.

Soft top 230. This rather more unusual and desirable variant has the advantage of a hood that is stowable inside the car, resulting in a neat, well finished appearance when down.

Left, a 230 with the hood down. The double skinned sills are a plus point. Below, the 230's engine with brake servo in foreground. Right, driving compartment of a 280 with automatic transmission.

MERCEDES-BENZ 230-SL AUTOMATIC

The comforts of home for the dignified sport

SOME CARS ARE easy for our staff to evaluate; they're better or worse than their contemporaries, or about the same. They may be ordinary in most respects and outstanding in one. The Mercedes-Benz 230-SL is not one of those cars as there really is no other comparable car.

For one thing, it takes considerable head-scratching to decide just what the 230-SL is. Is it a sports car? A Teutonic Thunderbird? The ultimate in GT? Defining the term "sports car" is as difficult as ever, though we think most will agree that the definition no longer needs to include "uncomfortable, hard-riding and noisy" as qualifications. Whatever the 230-SL is—perhaps a standard classification would be unfair—it is certainly individual; not quite like anything else on the road.

What really sets this car apart is its glorious road manners. It is surely the world's most advanced production car in this department. There is an old school of chassis design in which stiff springs are considered necessary to get good handling. Then there is a new school, which knows how to combine ride with roadability. The 230-SL combines these two qualities to a greater degree than any car we've driven. The combination to it all is fourfold: 1) a very rigid body-frame unit structure, 2) soft, supple suspension springs, 3) near-ideal wheel geometry and 4) large, radial-ply tires. We went charging over really horrendous road surfaces—including 3-in. potholes, severe dips and such—at speeds that would have either jarred our teeth out or sent us off course in most cars. This Mercedes simply goes on, never complaining, with hardly a creak and never a rattle from its open body—only the pitter-pat of its paw-like wheels, conforming to whatever they encounter.

Then there's the handling. Our car was equipped with Mercedes' power steering, which must be the finest example of this sometimes-disturbing device. One staff member, after driving some 30 miles in the car, was asked how he liked the power steering. His answer: "Oh, does it have power steering?" The effect is that of very easy unassisted steering, and to us this seems ideal. The feel is all there, and there's no question of inadequate feedback. As for cornering power itself, only a superlative adjective will do. We headed for our favorite winding road, which is not bump-free either, and found it impossible to get into any trouble. The car is a mild understeerer, and remains so until the rear is broken away by power—which is very tough to do. Suspension geometry is designed so that the rear wheels are poised for slightly better adhesion than the front ones; this in addition to the mild forward weight bias assures the understeer condition. The radial tires—German Firestone Phoenix by name—are pretty fat at 185-14 and have a very grippy tread design. So grippy they are, in fact, that they whine just like snow tires all the time, and whine even more loudly on

MERCEDES-BENZ 230-SL AUTOMATIC

AT A GLANCE...

Price as tested	$7367
Engine	6 cyl, sohc, 2306 cc, 170 bhp
Curb weight, lb	2905
Top speed, mph	115
Acceleration, 0-60 mph, sec	11.0
50-70 mph (4th-3rd gear), sec	7.2
Average fuel consumption, mpg	20

40

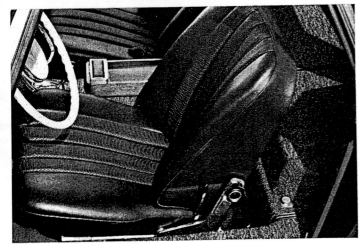

230-SL AUTOMATIC

corners. And they can be made to squeal loudly in violent cornering, but their bite always seems to be proportional to their bark.

Braking is another area in which this car really comes through. Pedal feel is, as with the steering, that of a light, unassisted system. Actually a power assist is standard on the car—necessitated by the particular design of the disc brakes in front and drums in the rear. In our simulated panic stops from 80 mph, there was no tendency for wheels to lock up or pull even with indiscriminate jabbing of the brake pedal. Instead, the car just hauled down at a rate of 30 ft/sec². Only after speed was reduced to the 25-mph range did anything unseemly begin to happen, and this was only a mild slewing from left to right. Nothing violent at all—except the deceleration rate. Six repeated stops from 80 at full tilt didn't noticeably fade the brakes, either. There was a moderate degree of nose dive, but nothing disturbing —the Mercedes front suspension has no anti-dive properties. We would judge that those big radial tires have just as much to do with the braking power of the car as they do with its cornering power, for we have driven other cars that seem to have equal brakes but cannot stop as well for lack of tire grip.

About the ride, handling and brakes we have nothing but unqualified praise. When it comes to the engine-transmission department, things get more complicated. The engine is probably the ultimate development of this series of Mercedes sohc sixes; it is a stretch of the 2.2-liter, as used in the 220 series, to 2.3 liters. At 170 bhp, it is very highly tuned, and uses fuel injection, among other things, to get its high specific output of 1.205 bhp/cu in. or 73.7 bhp/liter. The approach, then, is typically Mercedes: a small engine working very hard for its living, putting out a lot

of horsepower. Under way, the engine betrays its high-performance nature by being rather noisy and not particularly smooth. It is tractable—that is, it never bucks or responds unevenly—but very, very weak on low-speed torque. At highway speeds, it sounds rather busy.

Mercedes-Benz has approached the task of engineering an automatic transmission, as they approach most everything, in a most individual way. Very unlike other contemporary automatics, this is more like the old original Hydra-Matic: fluid coupling and a 4-speed planetary gearbox. The idea apparently was to give an all-out performance level very close to that of the manual 4-speed, a great deal of driver control over the gear changes and minimum loss in fuel economy. The result is the most controversial point about the car. There are three driving ranges: "4" gives a 2nd-gear start and upshifts at relatively low engine speeds to 3rd and 4th; "3" does the same except that it doesn't upshift to 4th; and "2" gives a 1st-gear start, upshifting to 2nd at high engine speeds. The shift quadrant, with a nice plastic-lined gate, is labeled 2340RP (0 is neutral) and works with much precision.

The most unfortunate part of the transmission's behavior, in our opinion, is the 2nd-gear start in range 4. Moving away from a stop, the response is extremely sluggish, almost like an old Buick Dynaflow in "Drive," and not until the engine reaches 1700 rpm does it begin to pull strongly. At that point, the engine surges ahead as if it had just gained a couple of cylinders. Meanwhile, you've been run over by that Volkswagen behind! The only alternative to this leisurely start, if you don't want to shift manually, is to floor the throttle and get a forced downshift to 1st gear—and go bounding away at full throttle, engine screaming. Exasperating. If you don't mind making that one manual shift, you can start off in "2" and make a nice, peppy start in first gear without going full bore.

Upshifts are about as positive as we can imagine, and vary from quite jerky at low speeds and light throttle openings to smooth at full throttle. Mercedes engineers have said that this gearbox will beat the fastest hand at making shifts, and we believe them. Automatic upshifts occur at 5600 rpm (1-2 shift in range 2) and about 6000 rpm for the others. The 1-2 shift cannot be delayed, but the others can be delayed to 6500 rpm, the engine redline, with some benefit to acceleration times. As you can see from the data panel, the four ratios in the automatic gearbox are quite widely spaced—they are the same as those used for the heavier sedans—and we think the car's behavior with the automatic could be improved by closer ratios and an automatic first-gear start in range 4. Or by about one more liter of engine displacement.

If there's one thing that a Mercedes is, it's comfortable. The seats on this 230-SL are among the finest we've seen anywhere. They're not pillowy—quite firm, they are contoured carefully and sufficiently adjustable to keep most anyone happy. The driving position brought no complaints from any staff member, and passengers felt at ease under all conditions. Interior materials are very Teutonic—the usual semi-carpet covering the central tunnel and luggage area behind the seats, with rubber mats in wear areas. Seats are upholstered in a combination of perforated and conventional vinyl, which should make for unusual comfort on hot days. Leather is available at $272.51 extra—a little surprising in view of the $6724 base price.

Most of the controls fall conveniently to hand (glaring exception is the headlight-parking light switch, which is a tough reach around or through the steering wheel to the left) and work smoothly. Little touches of convenience abound—like the 3-way control on the courtesy light under the dash that gives a choice of on, off or automatic operation with the doors; or the light on the outside of the glovebox door that lights maps or the floor below when open. A stalk on the left side of the steering column does a multitude of things and is quite handy once you're used to it. It operates the directional lights in the usual manner, a push to the right turns on the windshield wipers and another push turns them off (with the two speeds determined by a little slider switch on the face of the stick), and a push away from the driver works the windshield washer. Instruments are grouped in front of the driver, well lighted and legible. The heating/ventilating system is very complete and if its heat output lives up to the apparent thoroughness of its design, it should be adequate in the frigid climes of the North. There are separate temperature controls for the driver and passenger sides and even demister outlets for the side windows! The blower for the system is regulated by a rheostat, so that it's not limited to two or three speeds. Fresh-air ducts at the extremities of the dash panel complete the system.

On the safety side, aside from the car's obviously fine evasive capabilities, the steering column terminates just forward of the passenger-compartment bulkhead, minimizing its chances of being thrust into the driver's chest in a crash. Padded visors protect occupants' heads from the attaching toggles for the top over the windshield, and there is padding at the top and bottom of the dash, and in the center of the steering wheel. The seat backs are locked in place and must be released by a lever before they will swing forward. And the body follows the Mercedes graduated-rigidity principle.

Opinion about the car's styling was sharply divided among members of the staff. One thought it looked like a turtle too big for its shell, with the tires overhanging the main body panels; another found it clumsy; and another thought it was elegantly understated and ultra-contemporary. The top-to-lower body proportion is unusually large, and this seems to be the main point of contention in discussions of the 230-SL's appearance. It certainly makes for outstanding vision out of the car, whatever its esthetic effect. Especially with the hardtop in place this is one of the world's better cars for seeing what's going on outside. The hardtop itself, which is so well made and finished as to make one forget he is driving a "convertible" adds to the Tall Top feeling with its unusual roof panel; we've found very few people who find its appearance pleasing.

Interior styling is conservative and tasteful, with the exception of the steering wheel—about which we complained on the Mercedes 600. Real wood adorns the forward edge of the dash top, as well as the rear window surround on the hardtop. Additional pockets for maps, cigarettes, etc., are provided on each door, and a little tray between the seats is handy for often-used items. The whole effect isn't super-sumptuous, but rather the typical German presentation of luxury: a hard, monotone theme, with good materials.

The folding top doesn't quite measure up to the general quality standard. It looks good enough, but thrums a bit at highway speeds with the windows in any position but fully closed and also tends to bind the windows as they are being rolled up or down (which, incidentally, takes 6.3 turns of hard cranking). It isn't all that easy to put up, either, as bringing the positioning tabs into place over the windshield header takes more strength than most people can muster alone. It folds away quite easily, though, and is hidden very neatly by a cover panel.

One of our staff members suggested that the 230-SL might come closer than most any other car to meeting the approval of the American Medical Association as the ideal physician's express. It's a car of contrasts—thoroughly modern in its engineering but presenting a very conservative character; great-handling but not very fast. It imparts more security, real security, than most any car we know of, to its driver and passenger. And behind it all is the well-known Mercedes reputation for reliability and longevity. But at the price, we feel entitled to more performance in what is essentially a very sporting car.

Cowl intake feeds excellent ventilating system.

Large outlet supplies fresh air; small one is side window demister.

The 230-SL shows off its big, sticky tires, tasteful trim and beautiful finish.

ROAD TEST
MERCEDES-BENZ 230-SL AUTOMATIC

SCALE: 10" DIVISIONS

PRICE

List price.................$6724
Price as tested...........$7367

ENGINE

No. cylinders & type.......6 sohc
Bore x stroke, in.......3.23 x 2.87
Displacement, cc............2306
　Equivalent cu in.........140.7
Compression ratio..........9.3:1
Bhp @ rpm..........170 @ 5600
　Equivalent mph...........111
Torque @ rpm, lb-ft...159 @ 4500
　Equivalent mph............89
Fuel injection, make........M-B
　Type....................port
Type fuel required.......premium

DRIVE TRAIN

Transmission: M-B 4-speed automatic (fluid coupling with planetary gearbox).
Gear ratios: 4th (1.00).....3.75:1
　3rd (1.58)..............5.92:1
　2nd (2.52)..............9.45:1
　1st (3.98)..............14.9:1
Differential type..........hypoid
　Ratio..................3.75:1
Optional ratios...........none

CHASSIS & SUSPENSION

Frame type.......unit with body
Brake type...........disc/drum
　Swept area, sq in.........380
Tire size.................185-14
　Make & model Firestone Phoenix
Steering type.............power
　Turns, lock to lock.........3.2
　Turning circle, ft..........33.5
Front suspension: independent with
　unequal A-arms, coil springs,
　tube shocks and anti-roll bar.
Rear suspension: independent with
　single-pivot swing axles, coil
　springs, tube shocks and com-
　pensator spring.

ACCOMMODATION

Normal capacity, persons........2
Seat width, front, in........2 x 22
Head room..................40
Seat back adjustment, deg.....20
Entrance height, in..........50.5
Step-over height............14.0
Door width.................42.5
Driver comfort rating:
　For driver 69-in. tall........95
　For driver 72-in. tall........90
　For driver 75-in. tall........80
　(85–100, good; 70–85, fair;
　　under 70, poor)

GENERAL

Curb weight, lb............2905
Test weight................3275
Weight distribution (with
　driver), front/rear, %.....54/46
Wheelbase, in..............94.5
Track, front/rear............58.5
Overall length, in...........169
　Width..................69.3
　Height...........51.4 (50.8 ht)
Frontal area, sq ft..........20.2
Ground clearance, in..........5.5
Overhang, front/rear......28.5/44
Departure angle (no load), deg.16.4
Usable trunk space, cu ft......9.1
Fuel tank capacity, gal.......17.2

INSTRUMENTATION

Instruments: 140-mph speedometer, 7000-rpm tachometer, fuel,
oil pressure, water temperature,
clock, trip odometer.
Warning lights: ignition, high beam,
turn signal, heater-blower, handbrake on.

MISCELLANEOUS

Body styles available: roadster as
tested, fixed or removable hard
top.

EXTRA COST OPTIONS

Power steering, transverse occasional seat, whitewalls, leather
upholstery, etc.

CALCULATED DATA

Lb/hp (test wt).............19.2
Mph/1000 rpm (4th gear).....19.8
Engine revs/mi.............3030
Piston travel, ft/mi.........1450
Rpm @ 2500 ft/min........5230
　Equivalent mph..........103.7
Cu ft/ton mi...............75.2
R&T wear index............43.9

MAINTENANCE

Crankcase capacity, qt........4.8
　Change interval, mi.......2000
Oil filter type...........full-flow
　Change interval, mi.......2000
Chassis lube interval, mi.....2000

ROAD TEST RESULTS

ACCELERATION

	Auto	6500 shift
0–30 mph, sec.......	4.8	4.2
0–40 mph..........	6.7	5.9
0–50 mph..........	9.0	8.2
0–60 mph..........	12.0	11.0
0–70 mph..........	16.3	14.9
0–80 mph..........	23.5	20.3
50–70 mph (3rd gear)		6.6
Standing ¼-mi, sec..	18.4	17.7
Speed at end, mph.	74	76

TOP SPEEDS

High gear (5800), mph.......115
　3rd (6500)................81
　2nd (6500)................51
　1st (5600)................28

GRADE CLIMBING
(Tapley data)

High gear, max gradient, %....11
　3rd....................18
　2nd....................29
Total drag at 60 mph, lb......164

SPEEDOMETER ERROR

30 mph indicated......actual 27.0
40 mph.....................38.0
50 mph.....................48.3
60 mph.....................58.7
80 mph.....................78.3

FUEL CONSUMPTION

Normal driving, mpg........18–22
Cruising range, mi.......300–375

ACCELERATION & COASTING

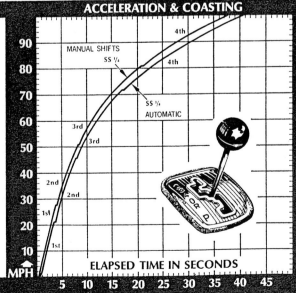

MANUAL SHIFTS
SS ¼
4th
4th
SS ¼
AUTOMATIC
3rd
3rd
2nd
2nd
1st
1st

ELAPSED TIME IN SECONDS
MPH
5　10　15　20　25　30　35　40　45
90 80 70 60 50 40 30 20 10

and a

handsome Mercedes 230 SL

The new car looks and handles as a sports Mercedes should.

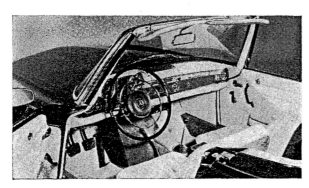

Interior shows that the 230 SL was built for comfort too.

SPECIFICATIONS
MERCEDES 230 SL

MOTOR: Six-cylinder, inline with single overhead cam-shaft and 9.3 to 1 compression. Bore 82 mm., stroke 72.8 mm., capacity 2306 c.c., 150 DIN h.p. at 5,500 r.p.m., 144.7 ft./lbs. torque at 4,200 r.p.m., 12 volt electrics, Bosch direct fuel injection with six-piston pump.

POWER TRAIN: Single-plate, dry clutch. Rear axle ratio 3.75 to 1. Gear ratios: First, 4.42 (3.98); second, 2.28 (2.52); third, 1.53 (1.58); fourth, 1.0 (1.0); reverse, 3.92 (4.15); with ratios for optional automatic box in ().

STEERING AND BRAKES: Recirculating ball steering, optionally with power booster (in conjunction with automatic gearbox). Girling disc front brakes, Mercedes rear drums. Swept area: discs 27.1 sq. in., drums 82.5 sq. in. Central handbrake on rear wheels.

WEIGHTS AND MEASURES: Wheelbase 94.5 in., front/rear track 58.5/58.6 in., length 168.7 in., width 69.3 in., height 51.8 in., turning circle 33 ft. 6 in., dry weight 2,855 lbs., 185 x 14 banded tyres. Lbs./h.p. 19.0, h.p./cu. in. 1.1, top speed 125 m.p.h. (120 with automatic box), acceleration 0-60 — approx. 10 sec., fuel consumption 16-24 m.p.g. (factory figures).

Which is an obvious tie to the Mercedes 230 SL. It too is an expensive automobile, but only if your fabled uncle has yet to shake loose. For anybody with that sort of purse, the Mercedes is value for the money in spades. They have done far more than replace the 190 SL — Daimler Benz has produced a new kind of luxury sports tourer. You have to get this clear from the start because this is no sort of a sports car in the Ferrari GTO sense. You don't race this car, you use it to attract blond chorus girls with particularly acute appreciation.

Not just a replacement

The 230 SL is more than a replacement for the obviously outmoded 190 SL, it is a different series. The 190 lacked handling by modern standards so they took over the suspension system — low-pivot swing axles with compensating spring — of the 220 SE sedan and fitted it to the shorter wheelbase of a two seater. They also took over front discs and rear drums to assure that area.

While the 230 SL seems a bit pricey it would cost far more if Mercedes didn't use so many production parts, body panels aside. The brilliance of the thing is using them to make an individual automobile with its own character of high-speed touring in sedan comfort plus, exceptional performance, good handling and unique aspect.

Styling won't please all

Not all of us are going to like the combination of rounded front, knife-edged rear and "pagoda" roof line but only the passengers are really aware how much bulge is used in the portion forward of the windshield. It was necessary to accommodate the upright and tall six cylinder engine. Blending could be improved upon.

In ride the 230 SL falls between a sports car and a sedan — in other words they achieved precisely what was desired, a sports-tourer that is safer by a margin than its driver will need,

The "pagoda" style roofline gives the new Mercedes 230 SL an individual appearance which will not meet with favour everywhere.

without being so brisk you would be roughed about. In terribly tight turns taken very fast you can induce a bit of rear-end scrabble, bringing up another point. The standard car has about 1.5 too many turns lock to lock, and a series of hairpins reminds you this is really a fairly large and/or heavy automobile.

Power steering and an excellent automatic transmission

Mercedes has the answer to that — power-assisted steering on the model of their 300 SE sedan line where road feel is retained but work lightened. With this you aim the 230 SL with the wrists rather than hauling it through the esses with muscle. Unfortunately it only comes with the optional automatic gearbox right now, but this is less of a drawback than one imagines.

Daimler's idea of an automatic — also 300 SE model — is four speeds with no auto-override so you can hold any ratio by notching the central lever, until valves holler quit. That, incidentally, only happens far, far above the horse power peak of 5,500 r.p.m. Another thousand may not improve the product but it won't break it. Using the two-pedal car you can drive like a boy-Fangio or set it in drive and contemplate your partner; with steering ease. For once, in a two-seater, I found such a game attractive.

New fuel injection unit

The 2.3 litre engine, bored out from their 220 six-cylinder sedans moves from low to high revs like a turbine, with ample power for the automatic, or the torque to dawdle about in third or fourth manual and still skate into the distance when the spirit moves you.

A big contribution to this torque range comes from the revised injection system — different to that used on the sedans. Instead of intermittent injection into the ports they arrange

six pets to feed the cylinders direct, through the valve openings. Further power was gained by a two-branch exhaust system running right to the rear. Gear ratios, either manual or automatic, fit the engine perfectly, though the flexibility makes it hard to choose bad ones.

The 230 SL will touch an honest 125 m.p.h. manual) or top 120 with the automatic box which is more than most can use these days, sad to tell. More important, it gets there quickly and has power reserves for passing. It should be an eminently rapid point-to-point car in daily traffic, leaving its occupants easy at the end of a hard day's motoring.

Either of these European Spring specials will do a modern job superlatively — naturally in different realms — and both are the kind of automobile you can drive many seasons, secure in the thought that the neigbours still envy you for superior automotive knowledge.

Fuel injected 2.3 litre powerplant gives a genuine 125 m.p.h.

MERCEDES BENZ 250 SL

RELEASED

AS might have been suspected for some time, the latest seven-main-bearing Mercedes 250 engine will now be fitted to the sports two-seater instead of the four-main-bearing 230 unit, as we reported last week. This changes the type number of the car from 230 SL to 250 SL and the capacity goes up from 2,306 to 2,496 c.c.

To enlarge the engine the stroke has been increased from 72·8 to 78·8mm, the bore staying at the same 82mm. This change does not affect the maximum power, which is still 150 b.h.p. net at 5,600 b.h.p., but peak torque is up from 145 to 159 lb. ft. at 4,500 r.p.m. Bosch six-plunger fuel injection to the ports is standard, of course.

The effect of this change is to improve acceleration by a worthwhile percentage and also to put the top speed up slightly; peak power revs have risen from 5,500 to 5,600 r.p.m. From rest to 60 m.p.h. is claimed now to take under 10sec with the manual gearbox (10·7sec in our Road Test of the 230 SL published on 4 September, 1964), and top speed is 124 m.p.h. for the manual version and 121 m.p.h. for the automatic (120 and 118 m.p.h. respectively for the 230 SL).

There is a practical choice of bodywork with the 250 SL which comes with a soft folding hood, detachable hardtop instead, or both together. Prices for these three versions have all been increased by £125 to between £3,611 and £3,806 and there are further options of Daimler-Benz 4-speed automatic transmission (£198) and power steering (£93). The automatic shift is a neat floor lever with full over-ride control.

Left: There are no changes to the interior on the new model

Right: The exterior still looks the same too, but the new engine improves the acceleration and top speed

Mercedes-Benz 250 SL

More displacement, more main bearings, more disc brakes.
And more pure, unadulterated driving pleasure.

Every driver who has more than a purely utilitarian interest in automobiles should drive a Mercedes-Benz 250 SL at least once in his life. The car is an almost perfect yardstick against which to measure any other car. There are cars with better acceleration, cars with better brakes, cars with better roadholding. But there is no car we can think of that has such a remarkably good balance of performance, safety, and comfort, and has them in such an absolutely civilized structure.

Civilized is the proper word. There is no category in the C/D Check List for "driving environment"; if there were we would have to come up with a super-excellent rating for the 250 SL. That's what Mercedes-Benz does best—provide an overall environment that makes the driver's job as pleasant and enjoyable as possible. And Mercedes-Benz does the job better in the 250 SL than in any of their other products.

We hadn't tested an SL (SL for "super" and "light"—at 3059 lbs., a bit of poetic license) since the intro-

duction of the 230 SL, back in June, 1963. Four years is a long time in present-day automotive evolution, and it is a measure of the Teutonic thoroughness with which Mercedes-Benz prepares a product for the market that the 230 SL had remained almost totally unchanged since its introduction.

Now, with the 250 designation, the SL gains the 2.5-liter, 7-main-bearing sohc six from the 250 sedan series, and 4-wheel disc brakes to replace the disc-and-drum set-up of the 230 SL. Period. With the brake change comes a balance valve between front and rear brakes, to help prevent rear-wheel lock-up under hard braking; with the extra 200cc of the new engine comes an increase in torque of approximately 10%. That's all the change there is, and it's almost undetectable. The increased torque makes no appreciable change in acceleration times, even though there is a marked feeling of increased power in the mid-range (as when passing). The new brakes are excellent in almost every case, but the old

system was already damned good.

That is an objective evaluation, but good cars always have a subjective effect. The 250 SL was a revelation, even for C/D staff members with relatively extensive 230 SL time. One by one, the staff members would come back to the office after a test drive in the 250 SL, and be asked, "How is it?" The answer was always, "Great! You try it," and the process would be repeated until the decision was unanimous.

The answer "Great!" has to have a lot to do with environment. We've never verified it at the factory, but one Mercedes-Benz type in New York tells us that whereas most other manufacturers tune out interior noise and harmonic vibrations up to about 70 mph, Mercedes engineers do the same thing up through 100 mph. The result is a solid, silent, acoustically "dead" structure that, at almost any conceivable speed, permits no distractions from the essential business of driving the car. Couple that with almost obsessive attention on Mercedes' part to transmitting all the *useful* sensory information about driving, and you begin to get a picture of what driving a 250 SL is like.

The useful information comes through subtly but firmly. The controversial "pagoda" roof of the 230-250 SL has been the subject of much discussion, but it does promote spectacular vision for the driver, with all kinds of window glass and almost no corner posts at all. The interior noise level is remarkably low, permitting normal conversation—or, wonder of wonders, listening to the radio at normal volume—at 100-mph speeds. Still, engine noise comes through well enough to provide that traditional Mercedes-Benz drone of assurance, and to give ample warning if you happen to be too far out of the proper rev range.

The steering in our test car was the excellent power system we've

PHOTOGRAPHY: GENE BUTERA

praised in the past on other Mercedes-Benz models. A certain meaningful amount of effort is necessary—in fact, just about the same amount required to handle the non-power steering of a much lighter car. For parking and slow maneuvers, the effort is light enough, yet road feel is practically unaltered.

Aside from these aspects—sight, sound, and road feel—there is still more shoring up of driver confidence, perhaps as much as anything the result of the 250 SL's extreme stability. Any maneuver is accompanied by a change in the car's attitude—either fore-and-aft or side-to-side—which can quickly be observed from the driver's seat. There is body lean under side loading, and there is an appreciable amount of nose dive when braking. But in any case, it is a smooth transference, a slight "cocking" that is absolutely predictable and completely reassuring. The car doesn't lurch; it simply cants, and it feels as stable in the canted position as it did when dead level.

These characteristics make it great fun to horse around with the 250 SL; to yank it off a straight line, punch the throttle in hard turns, brake at the wrong times, etc. The relatively heavy weight, the high polar moment of inertia, the extreme wide track (58.5 in.), and the healthy amount of rubber on the ground all combine to make the 250 respond with absolute dignity. It seems to tell you that it would never be so bad-mannered as to bite the hand that over-controls it.

Last month we tested a Ferrari 330/GTC, and the comparison of the two cars is interesting. At roughly $16,000, the Ferrari is just about as far as you can go in automotive sophistication. It has a rear-mounted 5-speed transmission, fully independent rear suspension, sohc V-12 with gobs of horsepower, and on and on.

The only thing remotely "far out" in the 250 SL's specifications, by contrast, is its fuel injection. The rest (in-line water-cooled six, albeit overhead-cam; swing-axle rear suspension, albeit low pivot; standard 4-speed manual or optional automatic transmission, etc.) are conventional if not old-fashioned. Yet it is difficult to appraise the 250 SL in terms of its mechanical components; the matching and blending of them is done too well. Whereas the Ferrari is designed, rightly so, for all-out, hair-raising performance, surrounded by a kind of rough-hewn, brutal luxury, the 250 SL is infinitely subtler. Its performance is in no way startling, yet it is capable of over-the-road averages that are limited in most cases only by the law.

Similarly, the luxuriousness of the car is in total effect. Detail work is very good, with leather in obscure places, chrome plates on thresholds, everything operational and heavy, solid, bank-vaultish. The test car had the removable hardtop, and the fit was so good that it was hard to believe that it was actually removable. Everything *fits,* everything *works.* The "orthopedic" design of

Mercedes-Benz seats is an unyielding Procrustean bed, on first impression, and there is a similar stern quality about the rest of the interior. There's no nonsense about German luxury, no sir.

The seating is very good, if you happen to fall within the accepted physical measurements that Mercedes used in designing it. The excellent shape makes the apparent hardness of the first impression quickly disappear. The seats are high—chairlike, in contrast to those of most low-slung sports cars. The back is adjustable for rake, and of course there is plenty of fore-and-aft movement—more than necessary, really. The non-adjustable steering wheel is positioned high, and angled from the vertical to suit the high seating position.

This seating-steering wheel relationship, plus our test car's automatic transmission, made for instant familiarity. Remember, again, last month's Ferrari, which positively daunted the more timid driver on first acquaintance. The 250 SL was the precise opposite. A half-dozen times we let non-enthusiast friends try the car, people unfamiliar with sports cars and unaccustomed to the responsibility of herding around $7000 cars. Without exception they would slide into the seat and drive away in complete confidence and control. That's when we began thinking about driver environment, as practiced by Mercedes-Benz.

The automatic transmission has a floor-mounted control lever, which works through a 2-3-4-0-R-P quadrant. On normal starts the shift from first to second is so early and so smooth that one gets the impression that it's a 3-speed box. Place the lever in any numbered slot other than "4" and you hold the transmission in that gear until you decide to take it out, which makes it quite possible to run over the 6500-rpm red line of the extremely smooth engine. Down-shifting is possible, although with a certain time lag in the process (and quite frequently, a great chirp from the rear wheels). The shifts under hard acceleration weren't the smoothest we've ever felt, but butter-smooth-

ness in that department would've been out of character, anyway.

One feature of the drive train we did object to was the choice of rear axle ratio. The 3.92 ratio that comes with the automatic is too high. With only 18.7 mph per 1000 rpm, you're turning 3200 at 60, and 5350 at 100 mph. It's a tribute to the sound deadening of the car that 100-mph cruising speeds aren't particularly fatiguing, but your ears are conscious of an electric motor-like

humming from the engine compartment. At the expense of some mid-range acceleration, you can get a 3.58 ratio with the manual 4-speed, and there is a special-option 5-speed ZF transmission which, with an overdrive 5th gear of 0.85:1, gives an effective cruising gear of 3.49. We'd recommend it, except that it takes forever to get and costs an extra $464.

MERCEDES-BENZ 250 SL AUTOMATIC

Importer: Mercedes-Benz of
North America
158 Linwood Plaza
Fort Lee, New Jersey

Number of dealers in U.S.: 240

Vehicle type: Front-engine, rear-wheel-drive, 2-passenger touring/sports car, all-steel integral body/chassis

Price as tested: $7715.00
(Manufacturer's suggested retail price, including all options listed below, Federal excise tax, dealer preparation and delivery charges; does not include state and local taxes, license or freight charges)

Options on test car: AM/FM radio ($170.00), power steering ($200.00), whitewall tires ($45.00), tinted glass ($46.00), floor mats ($15.00)

ENGINE
Type: Water-cooled 6-in-line, cast iron block, aluminum head, 7 main bearings
Bore x stroke..3.23 x 3.10 in, 82.0 x 78.8 mm
Displacement.............152.3 cu in, 2496 cc
Compression ratio..................9.5 to one
Carburetion.......Port-type fuel injection
Valve gear.......Chain-driven single overhead camshaft, rocker arms
Power (SAE)...............170 bhp @ 5600 rpm
Torque (SAE)........173.6 lbs/ft @ 4500 rpm
Specific power output.........1.11 bhp/cu in, 68.2 bhp/liter
Max. recommended engine speed...6500 rpm

DRIVE TRAIN
Transmission.............4-speed automatic, fluid coupling
Final drive ratio...................3.92 to one

Gear	Ratio	Mph/1000 rpm	Max. test speed
I	3.98	4.7	28 mph (6000 rpm)
II	2.52	7.4	48 mph (6500 rpm)
III	1.58	11.7	76 mph (6500 rpm)
IV	1.00	18.7	112 mph (6000 rpm)

DIMENSIONS AND CAPACITIES
Wheelbase............................94.5 in
Track...................F: 58.5 in, R: 58.5 in
Length..............................168.7 in
Width...............................69.2 in
Height..............................51.9 in
Ground clearance.....................4.9 in
Curb weight........................3059 lbs
Test weight........................3370 lbs
Weight distribution, F/R..........52.5/47.5%
Lbs/bhp (test weight)................19.8
Battery capacity..........12 volts, 55 amp/hr
Generator capacity.................490 watts
Fuel capacity......................21.7 gal
Oil capacity........................6.0 qts
Water capacity.....................13.5 qts

SUSPENSION
F: Ind., unequal-length wishbones, coil springs, anti-sway bar
R: Ind., low-pivot swing axle, trailing arms, coil springs, compensating spring

STEERING
Type.........Power-assisted recirculating ball
Turns lock-to-lock.....................3.0
Turning circle.........................34 ft

BRAKES
F...................10.7-in vented discs
R...........11.0-in vented discs, integrated drum-type parking brake
Swept area.....................421.1 sq in

WHEELS AND TIRES
Wheel size and type.....6.0J x 14-in, stamped steel, 5-bolt
Tire make, size and type....Firestone Phoenix 185 HR 14, radial ply, tube-type
Test inflation pressures..F: 30 psi, R: 32 psi
Tire load rating.....1160 lbs per tire @ 24 psi

PERFORMANCE
Zero to	Seconds
30 mph	3.2
40 mph	4.6
50 mph	7.0
60 mph	9.5
70 mph	12.4
80 mph	16.4
90 mph	20.9
100 mph	27.5

Standing ¼-mile..........16.9 sec @ 81 mph
80-0 mph panic stop.........250 ft (0.85 G)
Fuel mileage...18-22 mpg on premium fuel
Cruising range...................390-477 mi

MERCEDES-BENZ 250 SL
automatic
Top speed, estimated   118 mph
Temperature   53°F
Wind velocity   10–15mph
Altitude above sea level 43 ft
In 4 runs, 0 — 60 mph times
varied between
9.5 and 9.8 seconds

ENGINE
Starting.......................Good
Response.......................Good
Vibration...................Excellent
Noise..........................Good

DRIVE TRAIN
Shift linkage...................Good
Shift smoothness................Fair
Drive train noise...............Fair

STEERING
Effort......................Excellent
Response....................Excellent
Road feel...................Very Good
Kickback....................Very Good

SUSPENSION
Ride comfort................Very Good
Roll resistance.................Good
Pitch control...................Good
Harshness control...........Very Good

HANDLING
Directional control.........Very Good
Predictability..............Excellent
Evasive maneuverability.........Good
Resistance to sidewinds.........Good

BRAKES
Pedal pressure..............Very Good
Response........................Good
Fade resistance.............Excellent
Directional stability...........Good

CONTROLS
Wheel position..................Good
Pedal position..............Very Good
Gearshift position..........Very Good
Relationship................Excellent
Small controls..............Very Good

INTERIOR
Ease of entry/exit..............Good
Noise level (cruising)......Excellent
Front seating comfort.......Very Good
Front leg room..............Excellent
Front head room.................Fair
Front hip/shoulder room.....Very Good
Instrument comprehensiveness...Very Good
Instrument legibility.......Very Good

VISION
Forward.....................Excellent
Front quarter...............Excellent
Side........................Excellent
Rear quarter................Excellent
Rear........................Excellent

WEATHER PROTECTION
Heater/defroster............Excellent
Ventilation.................Excellent
Weather sealing.............Excellent

CONSTRUCTION QUALITY
Sheet metal.................Excellent
Paint.......................Excellent
Chrome......................Excellent
Upholstery..................Excellent
Padding.....................Very Good
Hardware....................Excellent

GENERAL
Headlight illumination......Excellent
Parking and signal lights.......Good
Wiper effectiveness.........Excellent
Service accessibility.......Very Good
Trunk space.....................Fair
Interior storage space......Very Good
Bumper protection...............Good

We should mention, also, that the new braking pressure regulator, which is intended to balance front and rear braking, wasn't quite up to the task on our test car. During our brake tests we did get some rear-wheel lockup. For normal driving, however, the brakes were extremely good. The power brake system makes the pedal seem touchy at first; the unusually light pedal pressure required, and the tremendous amount of rubber that those great big 185 x 14 Firestone-Phoenix radial-ply tires are putting on the ground, causes an application of the brakes to feel as if the whole car had turned suddenly into one great big art-gum eraser.

The ventilation and heating system of the 250 SL is a perfect example of Mercedes-Benz' thoroughness. As well as we could determine, there are no less than eight different air passages, and nine separate hand-operated controls for them. With this array of decision-making devices, it is possible to direct any given temperature of air, from frigid to fiery, in any quantity from a zephyr to a breath-taking blast, at any given spot from the driver's left little toe to the back of the passenger's head. The only problem is that it takes about 2000 miles of familiarity with the car to get the system completely deciphered.

And that's what we did—2000 miles of enthusiastic familiarizing. Two C/D staffers put 1500 miles on the car on a single weekend, giving them a chance to live with the car under every condition imaginable short of race tracks and absolute blizzards. They reported back as fully sold on the car's overall excellence as the rest of us were from shorter, more intensive experience. They even racked up one 3-hour stint of turnpike driving at an 85 mph average, during which the occupant of the passenger's seat sat quietly reading a book (with very fine print) the entire time.

Maybe that's why the 250 SL seems so civilized. Fangio could never win a Mille Miglia in a car like this. But the average inbred aristocrat could drive it from Brescia to Rome and back to Brescia, pass just about everything in sight, post a remarkably high average speed for the trip, and never hear a murmur of complaint from the lady in the passenger seat: As a matter of fact, she'd probably never even lift her nose out of her latest copy of Paris Match. And that's what we mean by civilized.

AUTOTEST

MERCEDES-BENZ
280SL (2,778 c.c.)

AT-A-GLANCE: Expensive two-seater tested with optional automatic transmission and power steering. 280 engine gives much improved performance, but revs hard and sounds fussy. Ultra-light brakes show some fade. Firm ride. Well engineered hardtop and hood.

MANUFACTURER
Daimler-Benz AG,   Stuttgart-Untertukheim, West Germany.

UK CONCESSIONAIRES
Mercedes-Benz (Great Britain) Ltd, Great West Road, Brentford, Middlesex.

PRICES
Basic	£3,564	0s	0d
Purchase Tax	£1,091	6s	0d
Seat belts (approx.) . . .	£14	0s	0d
Total (in GB)	£4,669	6s	0d

EXTRAS (inc PT)
Power steering*	£109	13s	0d
Automatic transmission*	£220	13s	0d
Tinted glass all round* .	£28	5s	0d

* Fitted to test car

PRICE AS TESTED . . £5,027 17s 0d

PERFORMANCE SUMMARY
Mean maximum speed	121 mph
Standing start ¼-mile	17.0 sec
0-60 mph	9.3 sec
30-70 mph through gears	8.7 sec
Typical fuel consumption	20 mpg
Miles per tankful	360

Left: The steering wheel is large and the facia has only a painted metal finish, in the same colour as the bodywork. Above: the boot is larger than it looks, with space under the spare wheel as well as alongside it. Tools are inside the wheel cover

THIS is rather more than the regular Autotest because the car used was delivered to us new and we completed 5,000 miles before handing it back. We had hoped to give readers details of our running experiences, but such a mileage is little more than the breaking-in period for a car like a Mercedes and even though it was compacted into a period of only six weeks, there was absolutely no trouble on which to report.

For the first 600 miles there were severe restrictions on the speeds in all gears, but from then on to about 1,200 it was possible to build up until the full performance could be used. To be honest, this was a frustrating business with a car of the 280 SL's potential, and we suffered from quite bad plug fouling in the early stages. As soon as maximum revs could be used there was no more trouble, except very occasionally after several days in heavy traffic.

In addition to the usual test procedure and general staff use the test car went on a trip to Italy and abroad again on a different visit to Spa in Belgium. We used the car for its intended purpose—high speed touring in the grand manner—much more than is usually possible, and were lucky enough to cover the majority of our mileage in fine weather with the hardtop at home in the garage and the soft hood folded away under its metal tonneau.

Under these conditions the 280 SL really comes into its own, being one of the quietest and most draught-free open cars we have ever driven. The usually cumbersome business of erecting the hood is so simplified on the

52

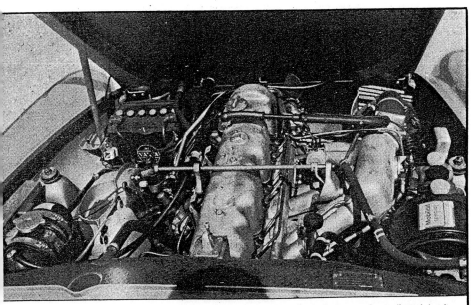

Above: the six-cylinder engine with its mechanical Bosch fuel injection looks large and complicated, but it all fits reasonably under the bonnet. Below: The 280 SL in open trim on the Grimsel pass in the Swiss Alps

Mercedes that it is no chore to put it up each time you park the car. Full length tonneau covers are much more fiddly in our experience, and if it should rain they allow the inside of the screen to get wet and still leave you with the problem of getting the hood up, if the rain is more than a passing shower.

The optional hardtop is a heavy steel structure, which takes two men to remove or replace. It is a precision fit on the body and gives much better three-quarter rear vision than the soft hood, which has blind panels at its corners. In effect the hardtop costs £189 extra, although you can buy the 280 SL as a coupé (hardtop, but no hood), convertible (no hardtop) or a coupé-convertible (soft and hardtops).

Other listed options are power steering and automatic transmission, our car being fitted with both, plus the added luxury of tinted glass (£28 5s extra including that in the hardtop). Having tried a 280 SL some years ago without the power steering and automatic, we reckon they are an essential part of the package.

This Mercedes sports car started out at the end of 1963 as the 230 SL with 2,306 c.c. engine and 150 bhp net. At the beginning of 1967 the engine size was increased to 2½ litres as an interim stage before the 280 version was announced in January 1968. Our test records show a lapse of six years since we reported on one in full, so this Autotest is long overdue.

Compared with that original 230 SL automatic, the 280 SL is a lot quicker. The latest engine develops 170 bhp (DIN) and considerably more torque than the 2.3 version. Slightly lower gearing (3.92 final drive instead of 3.75) enables the most to be made of the larger engine which is beefier and revs more.

Rapid acceleration

Thus we were able to take the 280 SL up to 6,500 rpm in second and third—first changes up automatically at 5,800 rpm with no over-riding provision—to advantage when measuring the acceleration. Compared with the 230 SL, the bigger-engined car was over 2sec quicker to 60 mph (9.3 against 11.4sec) and 4.3sec quicker to 100 mph (30.6 against 34.9sec). Over the standing quarter mile the latest car was 1.1sec faster, with a terminal speed 5mph higher (81 instead of 76 mph). On top speed the 280 SL recorded a mean and best of 121 mph (230 SL: 118 mph and 119 mph respectively) at which point the rev counter was in the red at 6,500 rpm.

Left to its own devices, the automatic gearbox (Mercedes' own, with four speeds and no torque convertor) changes up at lower speeds and adds 2.8sec to the 0 to 100 mph acceleration time.

The pattern of the manual selector is familiar, with park, reverse, neutral and three drive positions labelled 4, 3 and 2. In 4, all gears operate according to load, speed and throttle opening, while in 3 top is blanked off, and in 2 top and third are not allowed to engage. In addition to this simple and logical ruling, selecting 3 moves the maximum kickdown speed into second up from 25 to 37 mph, and selecting 2 enables the car to move off from rest in bottom without full throttle (in 3 or 4 it makes second gear starts unless the driver kicks down into bottom deliberately). In 2 also bottom can be obtained by kicking down at any speed up to 21 mph, and the change up to second takes place at 5,800 rpm instead of 4,000 rpm.

All this sounds very complex, but what it boils down to in effect is that when the driver wants more performance or more engine braking than normal, he selects a lower gear position, just as on a manual box. In the main the Mercedes brain-box does what the skilled driver would be doing had he complete control,

ACCELERATION

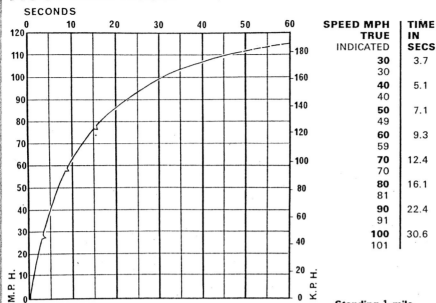

SECONDS

SPEED MPH TRUE INDICATED	TIME IN SECS
30	3.7
30	
40	5.1
40	
50	7.1
49	
60	9.3
59	
70	12.4
70	
80	16.1
81	
90	22.4
91	
100	30.6
101	

SPEED RANGE, GEAR RATIOS AND TIME IN SECONDS

mph	Top (3.92)	3rd (5.72)	2nd (9.37)	1st (15.58)
10-30	—	—	3.6	—
20-40	—	5.2	3.1	—
30-50	8.8	5.0	—	—
40-60	8.8	5.1	—	—
50-70	9.3	5.7	—	—
60-80	10.0	—	—	—
70-90	10.8	—	—	—
80-100	13.2	—	—	—

Standing ¼-mile
17.0 sec 81 mph
Standing kilometre
31.3 sec 101 mph
Test distance
4,998 miles
Mileage recorder
accurate

PERFORMANCE

MAXIMUM SPEEDS

Gear	mph	kph	
Top (mean)	121	195	6,
(best)	121	195	6,
3rd	82	132	6,
2nd	51	82	6,
1st	28	45	5,

BRAKES

(from 70 mph in neutral)
Pedal load for 0.5g stops in lb

1	20		6	35
2	20		7	37
3	20		8	40
4	30		9	40
5	35		10	40

RESPONSE (from 30 mph in neutral)

Load	g	Dista
20lb	0.40	
40lb	0.64	
60lb	0.94	
80lb	1.05	29
Handbrake	0.39	

Max. Gradient 1 in 3

MOTORWAY CRUISING

Indicated speed at 70 mph	70 r
Engine (rpm at 70 mph)	3,675
(mean piston speed)	1,945ft/r
Fuel (mpg at 70 mph)	23.5 r
Passing (50-70 mph)	5.7

COMPARISONS

MAXIMUM SPEED MPH
Porsche 911T	(£3,671)	129
Mercedes 280SL Auto	**(£4,876)**	**121**
Reliant Scimitar GTE	(£2,019)	117
Alfa Romeo 1750 GTV	(£2,431)	116
Triumph Stag	(£2,042)	115

0-60 MPH, SEC
Porsche 911T	8.1
Mercedes 280SL Automatic	**9.3**
Reliant Scimitar GTE	10.7
Alfa Romeo 1750 GTV	11.2
Triumph Stag	11.6

STANDING ¼-MILE, SEC
Porsche 911T	16.0
Mercedes 280SL Automatic	**17.0**
Reliant Scimitar GTE	17.4
Alfa Romeo 1750 GTV	18.0
Triumph Stag	18.2

OVERALL MPG
Alfa Romeo 1750 GTV	23.9
Triumph Stag	20.6
Mercedes 280SL Automatic	**19.0**
Reliant Scimitar GTE	18.5
Porsche 911T	17.9

GEARING (with 185-14in. tyres)
Top	18.6 mph per 1,000 rpm
3rd	12.7 mph per 1,000 rpm
2nd	7.8 mph per 1,000 rpm
1st	4.7 mph per 1,000 rpm

TEST CONDITIONS:
Weather: Fine and sunny. Wind: 7-15 mph. Temperature: 20 deg. C. (68 deg. F). Barometer 29.7 in. hg. Humidity: 44 per cent. Surfaces: dry concrete and asphalt.

WEIGHT:
Kerb weight: 27.8 cwt (3,120lb—1,415kg) (with oil, water and half full fuel tank). Distribution, per cent F. 53.4: R. 46.6. Laden as tested: 31.1 cwt (3,490lb—1,583kg).

TURNING CIRCLES:
Between kerbs L. 32ft 4in.; R. 32ft 11in. Between walls L. 34ft 1in.; R. 34ft 7in., steering wheel turns, lock to lock 3⅓.

Figures taken at 4,400 miles by our own staff at the Motor Industry Research Association proving ground at Nuneaton and on the Continent.

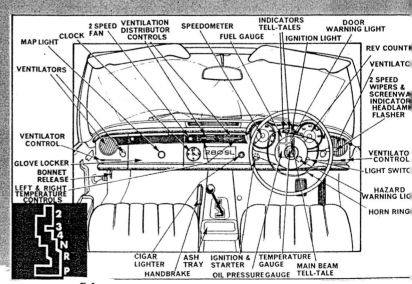

54

CONSUMPTION

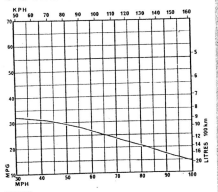

FUEL

(At constant speeds—mpg)

30 mph	. . . .	32.4
40 mph	. . . .	31.3
50 mph	. . . .	29.0
60 mph	. . . .	26.3
70 mph	. . . .	23.5
80 mph	. . . .	20.4
90 mph	. . . .	17.3
100 mph	. . . .	14.7

(Manufacturer's claimed figures; test car's fuel injection system incompatible with our test apparatus)

Typical mpg 20 (14.1 litres/100km)
Calculated (DIN) mpg 21.4 (13.2 litres/100km)
Overall mpg 19.0 (14.9 litres/100km)
Grade of fuel Premium, 4-star (min. 97 RM)

OIL

Miles per pint (SAE 30) 2,000

SPECIFICATION

FRONT ENGINE, REAR-WHEEL DRIVE

ENGINE
Cylinders . . . 6, in line
Main bearings . 7
Cooling system . Water; pump, viscous-coupled fan and thermostat
Bore . . . . . 86.5mm (3.41 in.)
Stroke . . . . 78.8mm (3.10 in.)
Displacement . 2,778 c.c. (169.5 cu.in.)
Valve gear . . Single overhead camshaft, finger tappets
Compression ratio 9.5-to-1 Min. octane rating: 96RM
Induction . . . Bosch mechanical fuel injection
Fuel pump . . . Bosch electric
Oil filter . . . Full flow, renewable element
Max. power . . 170 bhp (net) at 5,750 rpm
Max. torque . . 177 lb.ft (net) at 4,500 rpm

TRANSMISSION
Gearbox. . . . Daimler-Benz 4-speed automatic with fluid coupling
Gear ratios. . . Top 1.0
Third 1.46
Second 2.39
First 3.98
Reverse 5.47
Final drive . . . Hypoid bevel, ratio 3.92-to-1

CHASSIS and BODY
Construction . . Integral, with steel body

SUSPENSION
Front . . . . . Independent; double wishbones, coil springs, telescopic dampers
Rear . . . . . Independent; single-jointed low-pivot swing axles, coil springs, telescopic dampers

STEERING
Type . . . . . Daimler-Benz recirculating-ball, with power assistance
Wheel dia. . . . 16.9in.

BRAKES
Make and type . ATE discs front and rear
Servo—make
and type. . . ATE vacuum
Dimensions . . F 10.75 in. dia. R 10.28 in. dia.
Swept area . . F 229 sq.in., R 201 sq.in. Total 430 sq.in. (278 sq.in/ton laden)

WHEELS
Type . . . . . Pressed steel disc, 5-stud fixing, 6.0in. wide rim
Tyres—make . . Firestone
—type . . Pheonix radial ply tubed
—size . . 185 HR 14 in.

EQUIPMENT
Battery . . . . 12 Volt 55 Ah
Alternator . . . Bosch, 41 amp a.c.
Headlamps. . . Bosch asymmetric 90/80 watt (total)
Reversing lamp . Standard
Electric fuses . . 12
Screen wipers . 2-speed
Screen washer . Standard, electric, pedal-operated and linked to wipers
Interior heater . Standard, air-blending type
Heated backlight Extra
Safety belts . . Extra, anchorages built-in
Interior trim . . Pvc seats and headlining
Floor covering . Carpet
Jack . . . . . Screw pillar type
Jacking points . 4, underbody sides
Windscreen . . Laminated
Underbody
protection . . Pvc overall

MAINTENANCE
Fuel tank . . . 18 Imp. gallons (82 litres)
Cooling system . 22 pints (including heater)
Engine sump . . 10 pints (5.5 litres) SAE 30. Change oil every 6,000 miles. Change filter element every 6,000 miles.
Gearbox. . . . 6.6 pints Mercedes ATF. Change fluid every 30,000 miles
Final drive . . . 4.4 pints SAE 90 EP. Check level every 6,000 miles
Grease . . . . 18 points every 3,000 miles
Tyre pressures . F28:R33 psi(normal driving) F31:R36 psi (fast driving)
Max. payload. . 660 lb (300 kg)

PERFORMANCE DATA
Top gear mph per 1,000 rpm 18.6
Mean piston speed at max. power . . 2,970 ft/min
Bhp per ton laden . . . . 109.5 (net)

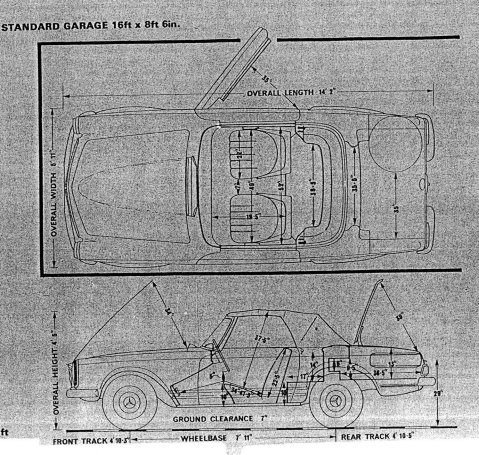

STANDARD GARAGE 16ft x 8ft 6in.

OVERALL LENGTH 14' 2"

OVERALL WIDTH 5' 11"

OVERALL HEIGHT 4' 5"

SCALE 0.3in. to 1ft

GROUND CLEARANCE 7"

FRONT TRACK 4' 10.5" WHEELBASE 7' 11" REAR TRACK 4' 10.5"

MERCEDES 280 SL...

with the main exception that it changes up much faster than he could ever hope to.

Sometimes it held on to a lower ratio longer than we would have liked, and with no torque convertor to cushion the drive line the quality of the kickdown changes was often rather jerky. In 1964 we said that this transmission was among the best in our experience and so it was. Since then, everyone else has improved theirs and even Mercedes have a better one, which surprisingly they do not fit to this car. By 1970 standards it is therefore only good in parts.

One of the reasons one notices the transmission so much is that the engine is rather small for the job it has to do and therefore sounds fussy when working hard. Cruising at only 100 mph, for example, puts the rev counter needle at about 5,500 rpm and even at a motorway 70 mph it shows almost 4,000 rpm.

Mechanically, from inside the car, the engine and gearbox are very quiet, most of the commotion seeming to come from the cooling fan even though it has a viscous coupling. The exhaust is quiet too, with a pleasant hum to it audible only with the car in open trim.

There is no doubt that the Mercedes power steering is among the best around, and it takes all the effort out of parking this car, which weighs over 1½ tons two-up with the hardtop in place. The 280 SL is very stable at speed in a straight line, but we found it needed small corrections when taking a sweeping bend at speed and lacked the positive feel of something like a Jaguar XJ6 or Aston Martin DBS. Just over three turns are needed between compact turning circles of close to 32 ft diameter.

Corners well

Driven hard on wet or dry roads, the car corners with virtually neutral characteristics, as long as the throttle is kept in a steady position. Lifting off on the apex of a tight turn causes the front to tuck in and stamping on it hard enough for a kickdown to take place sends the tail flicking out a few feet as the extra power thumps in. Under all normal conditions one can almost feel the fat radial tyres pressing down hard on the road and the low-pivot swing-axle rear suspension never did anything unwanted or unexpected.

By today's standards the ride is firm, with more bump thumping than on the larger Mercedes models. Hard, unyielding seats hold the occupants well with excellent grip around the hips, but they impart a certain numbness after a day spent in them.

Although we experienced no problems with the brakes on the road, they began to rumble towards the end of a hard stop from over 100 mph and faded noticeably during our repetitive tests from 70 mph. Initial brake reaction to low pedal efforts at slow speeds is fierce, and tends to take the driver by surprise in traffic. As the speed rises they become more progressive with a really hard, reassuring feel for very light loads. For most check braking less than 20 lb effort is required and it takes only 60lb on the pedal to get over 0.9g. Although this is an automatic car there is no provision for left-foot braking, the pedal being narrow and positioned in the normal place next to the accelerator.

The handbrake is down on the floor to the left of the tunnel (in the left-hand-drive position) and out of reach of the driver when he is wearing fixed seat belts. We preferred to use the much more handy transmission lock when parking. It held facing either way on the 1-in-3 test hill and stopped the car at 0.39g from 30 mph.

Mercedes have been using Bosch fuel injection for so long now (even the original 230 SL had it fitted) that it is to be expected that it should work reliably and faultlessly. Hot or cold we never had any problems starting the 280 SL and apart from the plug fouling already touched on it ran perfectly all the time. Idling seems quite fast, but it is only 650 rpm or so, and it does not cause too much creep.

Seatbacks have only a small range of rake adjustment and they cannot be reclined for sleeping. All our drivers below 6ft tall found the seat cushion a bit low, and the top of the large (17in.dia.) steering wheel obstructed forward vision slightly. Other than that the view out is excellent and the driver always feels well in command of his machine.

The instruments are set in a plain painted facia, with lots of bright chromium-plated fittings and numerals which are beginning to show their age now. On the left is the speedometer, reading to 140 mph and only 1 mph fast at 100 mph, and on the right is the dead accurate rev counter reading to 7,000 rpm. Between the two is a rectangular combination gauge containing three instruments and a set of warning lights. The oil pressure gauge was permanently up against its maximum reading stop under normal running conditions.

Wipers are controlled by the indicator st one press on the end to start them and anot to stop them. A little switch on the face of knob selects fast or slow speed and pushing whole lever away from the wheel squirts washers also. Pulling it up works the headla flasher. The dipswitch is on the floor.

The heater has a variable speed booster and individual temperature controls for ea side of the car. The fresh air vents at the e of the facia operate under ram effect or although little side-window demisting nozz are boosted by the heater fan.

We were glad to have the opportunity of s an extended mileage in this car, and it is to car's credit that it survived what turned out be something of an endurance test so well. I single day we covered 730 miles on Continent without any feeling of fatigue, a with the rev counter up around 6,000 rpm m of the time. Back home, speed limits and tra rule out that kind of a journey, but the 280 is none the less impressive in the way it stor past slower vehicles, slickly changing g instantaneously, with eager responses and a margin of safety always in hand.

At just over £5,000 it is far from cheap, a in a few ways it is beginning to show the age the original concept. Yet from behind the whe one somehow feels that in its engineering alo it is worth the money and at the top end of t two-seater market it has barely a single rival the world.

Above: The hardtop has obviously been designed to blend with the body styling. There are rubber inserts in the side rubbing strips and the special tyres have raised kerbing shoulders to protect their radial side walls

Left: No occasional seats behind, just a useful carpeted well

Below: Big wheels and fat tyres are the predominant features with nicely flared wheel arches. Rear quarter windows are fixed

MERCEDES-BENZ 280 SL

For those who value engineering finesse and high-

quality construction, it's alone in the field

SOME CARS don't change, they just get better. The Mercedes-Benz 280SL, latest version of a line that began as the 230SL in 1963, is the same as ever, just better. We always felt the 230SL was a great car but very short on torque and rather fussy in its performance, When the 250SL came along in 1967 the extra displacement gave a worthwhile boost in torque and the 7-bearing crankshaft meant a smoother, quieter engine; all-around disc brakes replaced the 230SL's disc/drum system at that time too. Now, with the 280SL, there's another good boost in torque plus a few minor changes, most of which are connected with safety and emission laws.

The primary change is a new cylinder block which raises displacement from 2496 cc to 2778 cc by a respacing of the cylinders and a concomitant bore increase from 82.0 mm to 86.5. Torque is up from 174 lb-ft at 4500 rpm to 193 at 4500,

power up from 170 bhp at 5600 rpm to 180 at 5700. For their home market in Germany, M-B put a hotter version of the 2.8 engine in the 280SL, developing 195 bhp at 5900 rpm, but to meet our emission laws they use a version with less valve overlap. Slightly revised fuel injection calibration, plus a fuel shutoff for deceleration above about 1500 rpm, also help the engine meet the standards.

Other changes evident in the latest model (these actually were incorporated in 1968 250SLs) include a revised steering wheel hub, energy-absorbing steering column, removable latch handles for the hard or soft top at the windshield, Kangol 3-point belts, improved lighting for the heater controls plus a "defrost" instruction plaque, a much-needed light in the shift quadrant, carpets on the front floors and "bag" door pockets instead of the rigid trays used before.

No question about it, the 2.8-liter engine comes on strong.

57

With the 4-speed automatic transmission, starting from rest in "4" range (2nd-gear start) is still leisurely because of the drag of a spring-applied band in the planetary gearbox at and just above idle, but once free of this the engine really pulls. Up through the gears it has enough acceleration for any traffic need, and top-gear acceleration is quite good from 35 mph on. Mercedes has decided that a 4.08:1 axle final drive is right for the American market, what with our highway speed limits, but with this ratio the SL sounds busy and seems never to be in top gear. This is a subjective objection; there is no question of durability with this gearing and the actual noise level isn't high when cruising—but if we were ordering a 280SL we'd ask for the 3.69:1 ratio and wait the extra month or so it would take to get it. The 280SL doesn't yet have the *new* automatic, which starts all the time in 1st gear and has better ratios: the 3.69 axle and this transmission would be the best combination, but we'll have to wait for that. In the manual gearbox department, a 4-speed is still standard, with the 5-speed ZF available at $464 extra. We feel the ZF should be standard as it has an overdrive 5th gear for more restful cruising as well as more satisfactory indirect ratios.

The 2.8 engine is mechanically smooth and has a nice exhaust note that, while a bit obtrusive at 45–55 mph in 4th, can be enjoyed to the hilt when revving up through the gears with the top down. The spark plugs were just a bit fouled from easy running when we arrived at Orange County Int'l

Raceway for our performance tests but cleared up after the first acceleration run. Fuel economy has suffered slightly, but the 280SL can still manage 19 mpg at "freeway" speeds and its 21.7-gal tank gives it a good cruising range.

In matters of handling, brakes and ride the SL is still one of the outstanding cars of the day. Certainly its (optional, but recommended) power steering is the best steering anywhere, giving the impression of just plain easy steering with no trickery about it. Handling is near neutral, with quick response to any steering input; but the single-pivot swing axles at the rear don't give quite the adhesion that a more up-to-date system would, so that it's easy to tweak out the rear end. The big, sticky Firestone Phoenix radial tires give fairly high cornering limits, but it's obvious that the added torque of the 280 engine brings this venerable suspension close to the end of its usefulness.

The ride, over all sorts of roads, is fantastic. The body is absolutely rigid and rattle-free, regardless of which top is installed, and the supple suspension just works away down there without disturbing the superb poise of the SL. Our test car had one ride peculiarity—a rather severe case of "freeway hop" in which the car gets to bounding like a basketball over the slightly humped concrete pavement segments at 65-75 mph—but a staff member's 250SL, with over 4000 miles on its odo, has shed this habit; presumably the shocks have to be broken in.

M-B's power-assisted disc brakes are a little touchy

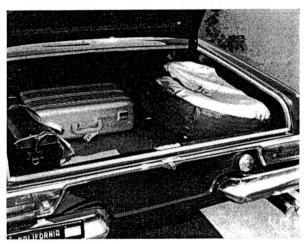

MERCEDES-BENZ 280 SL

at first but not at all tricky. Panic-stop capability of the 280SL is just equal to that of the disc/drum 230SL—an impressive 90%g—but fade resistance is improved and we got no fade at all in our 6-stop test (though there was slight pulling on the 6th stop). The brakes squeal occasionally, as do most discs, and the handbrake won't hold on a 30% grade—again a common shortcoming of discs. The 280SL still suffers from an excess of nosedive on braking, but this doesn't have any ill effects on its braking—just a bit of a bother.

The SL is perhaps the only sports car that gives a commanding driving position and view of the road. It's not a very low car, and its tall glass areas, relatively low beltline and visible corners make it one of the most maneuverable traffic cars we've ever driven in spite of its relatively large size. The steering wheel is just far enough away but a little too vertical for best support of the arms' weight; no adjustment is provided for it.

Mercedes seats are supposedly "orthopedically designed," and we're inclined to believe the claim. Their backrests are adjustable and they seem to give all the right support; the backrest adjusting knob, however, is hard to reach when one is seated and has the door closed. All controls are within easy reach but the passenger-side window can be a pain to raise or lower from the driver's seat—it takes almost six-and-a-half turns! The heating-ventilation system is comprehensive and effective, with separate left and right fresh-air vents and heater controls and a rheostat-regulated heater blower. However, there is not enough provision for flow-through (even though the HT has exits), what with the tight sealing of either hard or soft top, and one gets much better flow through the interior with a window cracked.

Noise level is exceptionally low with either top, even at speeds of 70–80 mph; the whining tires intrude a little and the busy engine makes a distant hum, but we don't know of a sports car that is as quiet overall. The hardtop—which was the only top this test car had—gives more rear vision than the soft top and fits precisely; it detaches with a turn of its four locking levers, but it does take two strong people to lift it off and carry it away.

Finish is another strong point of the 280SL, as you would expect at over $7000. Its paint is enamel, which means a rather noticeable degree of orange peel, but it is applied carefully and should be very durable. All chromework is lustrous and, with the exception of an ill-fitting right front carpet, we could find no flaws anywhere. Perhaps the trunk could be a bit more lavish at the price—it's only got a rubber mat on its floor and a spare tire cover. A good tool kit is provided.

The 280SL is a complex car, especially in the engine compartment with the mechanical fuel injection system looking like a graduate project at the Institute of Plumbing Engineers. But it is a well-proven, reliable car and the quality of its execution is a delight to the connoisseur of fine automotive machinery. It is somewhat paradoxical that this car does not offer the latest engineering developments of Mercedes-Benz—the improved automatic transmission, the anti-dive front suspension or the new semi-trailing rear suspension—but these probably won't be forthcoming for at least a year. In any case it is still a unique and desirable car; for those who have less than $10,000 to spend and value finesse, pure quality and drivability more than jazzy looks, it is alone in the field.

59

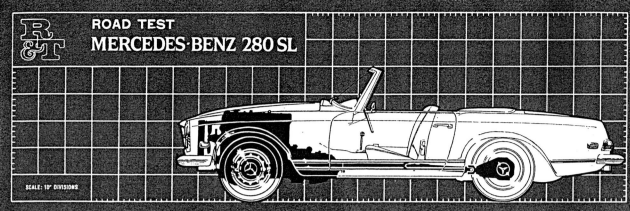

PRICE

Basic list. $6731
As tested. $7536

ENGINE

Type . . . . 6 cyl inline, sohc
Bore x stroke, mm. . . . .86.5 x 78.8
　Equivalent in. . . . . .3.41 x 3.10
Displacement, cc/cu in.2778/169.5
Compression ratio. 9.5:1
Bhp @ rpm. . . . . .180 @ 5700
　Equivalent mph. 100
Torque @ rpm, lb-ft. .193 @ 4500
　Equivalent mph. 79
Fuel injection . .Bosch—MB mechanical; port injectors
Type fuel required. . . . . .premium

DRIVE TRAIN

Transmission: 4-speed automatic (fluid coupling with planetary gearbox)
Gear ratios: 4th (1.00). 4.08:1
　3rd (1.58). 6.44:1
　2nd (2.52). 10.27:1
　1st (3.98). 16.21:1
Final drive ratio. 4.08:1
Optional ratios. 3.92, 3.69:1

CHASSIS & BODY

Body/frame: unit construction with steel & aluminum panels
Brake type: 10.8-in. disc front, 11.0-in. disc rear; auxiliary drum handbrake in rear discs
　Swept area, sq in. 430
Wheels. . . . . .steel disc, 14 x 6
Tires: Firestone Phoenix 185 HR-14
Steering type. . . . .recirculating ball, power assisted
　Overall ratio. 15.1:1
　Turns, lock-to-lock. 3.2
　Turning circle, ft. 33.5
Front suspension: unequal-length A-arms, coil springs, tube shocks, anti-roll bar
Rear suspension: single-low-pivot swing axles, trailing arms, coil springs, tube shocks

OPTIONAL EQUIPMENT

Included in "as tested" price: automatic transmission, power steering, AM/FM radio, tinted glass, whitewall tires
Other: 5-speed ZF gearbox, A/C, misc. minor items

ACCOMMODATION

Seating capacity, persons. 2
Seat width. . . . . .2 x 22.0
Head room. 40.0
Seat back adjustment, deg. . . .20
Driver comfort rating (scale of 100):
　Driver 69 in. tall. 95
　Driver 72 in. tall. 90
　Driver 75 in. tall. 80

INSTRUMENTATION

Instruments: 140-mph speedometer, 7000-rpm tachometer, fuel level, oil pressure, water temperature, 99,999 odometer, 999.9 trip odo
Warning lights: alternator, brake system, high beam, fuel level, directional signals

MAINTENANCE

Crankcase capacity, qt. 5.8
　Change interval, mi. 6000
Filter change interval, mi. . . . 6000
Chassis lube interval, mi 3000
Tire pressures, psi. 26/31

MISCELLANEOUS

Body styles available: roadster with soft top, hardtop or both tops
Warranty period, mo/mi :24/24,000

GENERAL

Curb weight, lb. 3120
Test weight. 3480
Weight distribution (with driver), front/rear, %. . . .53/47
Wheelbase, in 94.5
Track front/rear. 58 3/58.5
Overall length. 168.8
　Width. 70.0
　Height. 51.4
Frontal area, sq ft. 20.0
Ground clearance, in. 5.0
Overhang, front/rear. . .28.7/45.6
Usable trunk space, cu ft. 9.1
Fuel tank capacity, gal. 21.7

CALCULATED DATA

Lb/hp (test wt). 19.4
Mph/1000 rpm (4th gear). 17.6
Engine revs/mi (60 mph). . . . 3400
Piston travel, ft/mi. 1760
Rpm @ 2500 ft/min. 4840
　Equivalent mph. 85
Cu ft/ton mi. 96
R&T wear index. 60
Brake swept area sq in/ton. . . .248

ROAD TEST RESULTS

ACCELERATION

| Time to distance, sec: | 6500 |
	Auto	shifts
0–100 ft. 3.6		3.4
0–250 ft. 6.4		6.1
0–500 ft. 9.7		9.3
0–750 ft. 12.3		11.9
0–1000 ft. 14.6		14.3
0–1320 ft (¼ mi). .17.3		17.1
Speed at ¼ mi, mph. . 79		80

Time to speed, sec:

0–30 mph. 4.0		3.6
0–40 mph. 5.7		5.2
0–50 mph. 7.6		7.2
0–60 mph. 10.3		9.9
0–70 mph. 13.5		13.1
0–80 mph. 17.7		17.1
0–100 mph. 31.5		30.5

Passing exposure time, sec:
　To pass car going 50 mph. . . 5.5

FUEL CONSUMPTION

Normal driving, mpg. 16–19
Cruising range, mi. 345–410

SPEEDS IN GEARS

4th gear (6500 rpm), mph 114
3rd (6500). 73
2nd (6500). 45
1st (6000). 25

BRAKES

Panic stop from 80 mph:
　Deceleration, % g 90
　Control. . . . . .excellent
Fade test: percent of increase in pedal effort required to maintain 50%-g deceleration rate in six stops from 60 mph. . . . . .nil
Parking brake: hold 30% grade. no
Overall brake rating. . . very good

SPEEDOMETER ERROR

30 mph indicated. . . . . .actual 29.7
40 mph. 39.6
60 mph. 58.8
80 mph. 78.3
100 mph. 97.6
Odometer, 10.0 mi. . . . .actual 9.80

ACCELERATION & COASTING

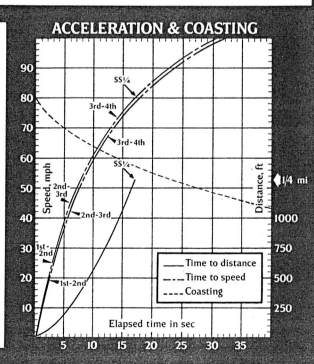

SS¼
3rd-4th
3rd-4th
SS¼
2nd-3rd
2nd-3rd
1st-2nd
1st-2nd

Speed, mph
Distance, ft
¼ mi
Elapsed time in sec

——— Time to distance
– – – Time to speed
· · · · Coasting

USED CAR TEST

1968 Mercedes-Benz 280SL automatic No. 335

PRICES

Car for sale at Basingstoke at	£3,450
Typical trade value for same age and model in average condition	£3,000
Total cost of car when new including tax	£4,487
Depreciation over 3 years	£1,487
Annual depreciation as proportion of cost new	10½ per cent

DATA

Date first registered	1 October 1968
Number of owners	2
Tax expired	30 September 1971
M.o.T.	September 1972
Fuel consumption	17-22 mpg
Oil consumption	2,000 mpp
Mileometer reading	40,862

PERFORMANCE CHECK

(Figures in brackets are those of the original Road Test, published 3 September 1970).

0 to 30 mph	4.0 sec	(3.7)
0 to 40 mph	5.4 sec	(5.1)
0 to 50 mph	7.1 sec	(7.1)
0 to 60 mph	9.2 sec	(9.3)
0 to 70 mph	11.6 sec	(12.4)
0 to 80 mph	15.6 sec	(16.1)
0 to 90 mph	19.4 sec	(22.4)
0 to 100 mph	25.3 sec	(30.6)
In top gear:		
30 to 50 mph	9.4 sec	(8.8)
40 to 60 mph	8.1 sec	(8.8)
50 to 70 mph	7.3 sec	(9.3)
60 to 80 mph	8.4 sec	(10.0)
70 to 90 mph	8.5 sec	(10.8)
80 to 100 mph	10.4 sec	(13.2)
Standing ¼ mile	16.9 sec	(17.0)
Standing Km	30.7 sec	(31.3)

TYRES

Size: 185HR14. Approx cost per replacement cover £15.50. Depth of original tread 9mm; remaining tread depth 3mm (left front and rear); 4mm (right front); 5mm (right rear and spare).

TOOLS

Complete kit in boot (in spare wheel). Handbook with car.

CAR FOR SALE AT:

Clover Leaf Cars Ltd, Basing, Basingstoke, Hampshire. Tel: Basingstoke 3896.

TO some people in Britain, Mercedes cars seem disproportionately expensive. Cars bearing the famous three-pointed star hold other Britons in almost legendary awe, which makes the prices charged for them in this country understandably high. A true impression is somewhere between the two. Daimler-Benz make an extensive range of cars ranging from what one might call the lower middle-class 2-litre diesels — which both knowledgeable Germans and Daimler-Benz themselves are quick to point out are their most important models and their bread and butter — through the worthy "middle" middle-class 250 petrol-engined models to that German aristocrat of the *autobahnen*, the great 300SEL 6.3. All, of whatever pretension, share one common quality; a high standard of design and workmanship.

This 280SL automatic seems to prove this point. At 40,000 miles it is one of the most impressive used cars we have met. Its performance equals that of the original Road Test car at the bottom end and beats it from mid-range onwards. The bodywork looks like

new. We were hard put to find any noticeable item amiss.

The power unit some of us thought quieter if anything than the original car, though that does not mean that it is all that quiet; there is the usual quite marked clatter from the injectors when idling, which itself becomes a little erratic once the car is warmed up properly. It is, of course, still a somewhat fussy car like its smaller-engined predecessors, though the extra capacity gives some real bite to the fuss from around 4,000 rpm onwards. The transmission has one of the nicest selectors of any automatic we know, and makes its changes as smoothly and as readily as it should. Its only small failing, characteristic of the car and not a fault peculiar to this one, is its preference for staying in 3rd instead of top "gear" when one is ambling along at 30 mph or so in town.

Happy to cruise at a comfortable 100 mph, the car's behaviour here is spoiled by one easily remedied fault — the perished rubber seal at the top of the driver's window just near his offside ear, which has to suffer a lot of wind noise. It is safe to assume that the vendors will

deal with this before sale. When first collected we noticed a slight pull to the right when cruising fast, but this diminished during the test period. High speed straight stability on smooth roads is excellent and around town one is very glad that at least *one* manufacturer who offers power steering had the sense to take advantage of the power to give you quite high gearing in the steering mechanism instead of the usual excessively low-geared set-ups. This makes the car very handy when rounding tight right-angle bends.

On bumpy roads there is just a suggestion of wander typical of the car; only the more sensitive drivers will notice it. Ride is an odd mixture of surprisingly sharp response to sharp edges like raised manhole covers, and good accommodation of longer lower frequency depressions.

Brakes are exceptionally light during ordinary town running, but pedal loads go up noticeably if one makes any frequent demands on them on open roads. The handbrake is awkward to reach, being on the far side of the fat transmission tunnel, but as the car is an automatic with provision for locking the gearbox, that doesn't matter much.

All controls are in perfect order. It is a car which you can mostly drive almost with the finger tips — thanks to the delightfully easy-moving combined winker-washer-two-speed wiper-flasher stalk, that old fashioned but still ideal arrangement, the horn ring, and a simple instrument panel. The lighting master switch is surprisingly simple on such a car (and no shame to Daimler-Benz for that), but is a bit awkward to reach.

Visibility is an example to nearly all other manufacturers; the car always seems what it is — wide, but no more so than the reality. Little details of construction — such as the simple yet very sturdy door holding-open arrangement — give pleasure to the engineering eye, and are too numerous to mention here. Under the bonnet it is heavy and ponderous in design, but nicely tidy. After the early part of its life when the service record shows that it was looked after by Mercedes-Benz (Great Britain) Ltd, it came under the mechanical care of the present sellers, who have obviously done their job conscientiously.

Quite often it is with relief that we hand bac used cars to the people selling them — no necessarily because the car is intrinsically poo but because its condition is alarmingly bad; it in such cases with even more relief that w finish the performance tests, thankful that th car has not failed in the process. We have ha not the slightest shadow of such reservation about this 280SL; its price is high, but if a car in such condition after this mileage then seems worth it. Some Mercedes fanciers ma agree with some of us that, with its classicall clean shape, the 280SL is in many ways a mor desirable car than its somewhat over-decorate and clumsier-looking bigger-engined descen dant.

CONDITION SUMMARY

Bodywork

One might suspect from the very clean state o the roof lining — and from a suggestion o what may be upholstery cleaner spilt in the ver useful little tray in the centre of the car — tha it had been a little stained. The only obvious thing amiss inside the car — but not a thing one notices right away — is the warped state o the loudspeaker fret, a wooden affair. We had difficulty persuading the push button clipping the optional back seat upright to hold Paintwork looks original and completely unblemished as far as we could see. There are no indications of any accident damage, either remaining or obviously covered up.

Equipment

The speedometer, entirely free from an shake in the needle, is only 3 per cent optimisti at 100 mph. All electrical equipment is in working order.

Accessories

A Motorola press-button tuned radio is fitted and works well enough except that its range in "shrouded" conditions is restricted and its loudspeaker distorts a little too readily at the sort of volume one needs to hear music properly at 80 mph odd.

ABOUT THE MERCEDES 280SL

The 280SL, now replaced by the vee-8 350SL, traces its ancestry back to the 190SL first introduced in 1954, which was a much gentler little brother (or perhaps one should say cousin, their characters being so different) to the fierce gull-wing doored 300SL. The 190SL used a four-cylinder shorter-stroke 1,897 c.c. version of the bigger car's six-cylinder 3-litre unit. Mercedes' famous low-pivot swing-axle rear suspension was used, being intended to avoid the vicious habits of ordinary swing-axles systems when cornered hard.

At the end of 1962 the 230SL replaced the 190, being a faster and more advanced car; it was notable for the replacement of the previous car's somewhat bulbous body with the extremely handsome squared-up shape still so good to look at today, and also the adoption of Bosch fuel injection. The 250SL gave more torque but the same maximum power, and appeared in March 1967. Its 2,496 c.c. engine was a longer stroke version of the 230SL one. The 280SL came on the scene in 1968, with a capacity of 2,778 c.c., and the same swing-axle rear end which has at last disappeared on the new 350SL in favour of trailing arms. ☐

Above: Car dealers are fond of the word"immaculate" when talking about secondhand-car condition, but few of their wares justify the word as does this Mercedes

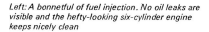

Left: A bonnetful of fuel injection. No oil leaks are visible and the hefty-looking six-cylinder engine keeps nicely clean

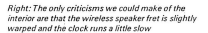

Right: The only criticisms we could make of the interior are that the wireless speaker fret is slightly warped and the clock runs a little slow

Mercedes-Benz 250SL

From hand-fitted body panels to final hand-sprayed enamel coat, the 250SL is meticulously assembled on one of the world's least frantic automobile production lines.

Exquisitely well built as it is, the 250SL is no brittle showpiece. It is a highly virile machine: "This combination of absolute security, complete stability, and plain old hell-raising fun must be driven to be believed," states *Car and Driver*.

Not a 300SL

The 250SL's road-holding abilities are almost inexhaustible. This smaller, lower car even eclipses the legendary 300SL in sheer handling prowess.

Some clues: the 250SL stands a mere 4 feet, 4 inches high—yet overall width is almost 6 feet. Its track is so wide-stanced that those chubby, 14-inch *radial ply tires* seem to bulge out from the body sides to straddle the pavement. You ride on a fully independent, low-pivot rear swing-axle suspension—a design proved on the world-champion 300SLR.

The 250SL's 4-wheel *disc* brakes stop you squarely, smoothly, without pulling or fading, even in repeated hard panic stops.

Mit Einspritzer

The 250SL is only stretched to its peak when the speedometer needle nudges 124 mph. You could level off at 100 mph and stay there until it became boring or illegal.

A 6-cylinder, single overhead camshaft engine turns the trick (while turning 6500 rpm). There are few stronger or more potent 2.5 liter engines known, and one secret is an *Einspritzer*—fuel injection

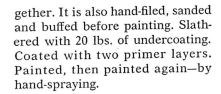

system. Another secret: a high-speed bench test before it leaves the factory.

Exotic but solid

At 3000 lbs., the 250SL is one of the world's most *solid* two-seaters. The body is welded up, not bolted to-

gether. It is also hand-filed, sanded and buffed before painting. Slathered with 20 lbs. of undercoating. Coated with two primer layers. Painted, then painted again—by hand-spraying.

Hardly Spartan

The 250SL may never qualify as a pure sports car, simply because it is too comfortable. You're cradled in a contoured, thickly padded driver's seat that resembles an armchair more than a typical sports car "bucket."

"They grip, support, relax and ventilate your body supremely well," reports Britain's *Motor* magazine of these seats. They also recline. Thousands of tiny holes in the upholstery material keep air circulating. Two slots on the rear of both backrests allow pent-up heat to escape from *inside* the seat structure.

Visibility in the 250SL is so airy it's almost eerie. You sit high. The car's waist is low. Side windows arch up over 15 inches. You watch the road ahead, not a vast expanse of hood. The psychological edge alone is worth an extra 5 mph.

You can actually pack luggage in this car. There is room for 7 cu. ft. of duffle in the trunk. You can stow another 5 cu. ft. in the carpeted area behind the seats.

Options

The world's best power-assisted steering and a remarkable, *4-speed* automatic transmission are two of the few optional extras you may feel you need.

There are 3 models to choose from: the Roadster, with convertible top; the Coupe, with an all-weather removable metal hardtop that neither feels nor looks removable; and the Coupe/Roadster, which offers both and is illustrated here.

Your authorized Mercedes-Benz dealer will be glad to furnish a 250SL for a thorough test run.

MERCEDES-BENZ 350SLC

Stuttgart's latest interpretation of the super-luxury coupe

JESSE ALEXANDER PHOTOS

 WE WERE A bit surprised when the Mercedes-Benz 350SLC was introduced, as we hadn't expected the successor to the old big coupe, which was based on a sedan, to grow out of the sports model. Actually, it's a little misleading to say the SLC comes from the SL, as they were designed simultaneously and planned from the beginning as a pair. But the SL appeared first, so it's a natural to consider it an SL that's been stretched some 14 in. in the middle. The extra metal makes the wheelbase and overall length that much longer and provides room for a rear seat and a slightly larger trunk. The SLC has a fixed roof whereas the SL has a folding fabric one and a lift-off hardtop. Otherwise the two are very much the same car. All front-end sheet metal is interchangeable as are the doors, most exterior hardware and most of the front passenger compartment. The windshield is a smidgen taller on the SLC, as is the overall height. The SLC is 150 lbs heavier than the SL with both its roofs—a modest weight penalty for an extra 2- to 3-person carrying capacity and the added trunk space. If the SL seems heavy for its size, the SLC does not and it was probably the SL structure that was overdesigned to provide for the extra length of the SLC.

Whatever the technicalities, the SLC is a high-style prestige car. Whether or not the styling—probably somewhat compromised for the interchangeability—is successful is a matter the R&T staff couldn't even resolve among itself. Some consider the SLC better-looking than the SL, others say some serious compromises were made in proportions. All agreed that the slatted, fixed rear sections of the quarter windows look odd, and we concluded that they might be an afterthought solution to an awkward area of the car. Longer quarter windows would not roll down because of interference with the wheel wells, and yet Mercedes always designs good all-around vision into its cars. So the slats may have been adopted merely to avoid

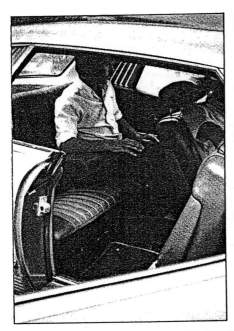

the look of a 2-piece quarter window and still give the driver an extra few inches of vision.

Like any prestige car, the SLC is full of gadgets—most of which serve a useful purpose. As it should at $15,000 (that is approximate; the price is not firm at this time), it has a long list of standard equipment: air conditioning, automatic transmission, power steering and brakes (discs all around), stereo AM-FM radio with electric antenna, the best available radial tires, leather upholstery, electric window lifts, heated rear window and fog lights. Beyond that are the little gadgets: a central vacuum system that locks the right door, trunk and gas cap when the driver's door is locked; vacuum-restrained seatbacks that lock when the engine is running and the doors are closed (but have pushbutton overrides for rear passengers), a timer for the rear window heat, a removable map light in the glovebox, door panels that are heated or cooled by the heating or air conditioning, and a lighting position that operates either the left-side or the right-side parking lights for parking on narrow, busy streets. The front seats have the usual Mercedes adjustable backrests, and in addition the track of the driver's seat can be raised or lowered.

As we mentioned in our test of the 350SL, ergonomics—which Funk & Wagnalls defines as "the study of the relationship between man and his working environment, with special reference to anatomical, physiological and psychological factors; human engineering"—were taken seriously in the layout of the interior and controls of these two models. The steering wheel is big, but by being so it clears the entire instrument cluster, which itself is extremely readable, and free from glare at night. And that wheel is the most fully padded one we've seen on any production car—itself a passive restraint device of the first order. Essential controls are near the steering wheel, are different from each other so there's no confusing them and, although they are so different from most other cars as to take some time for orientation, really clever and well thought out. There are two outside rearview mirrors, polarized and adjustable from the inside. Distribution of air from the climate control system is excellent, aided by those door ducts. And, for sheer entertainment value, the Becker Europa stereo radio in our test car was excellent in tone, separation and reception—it seems to have been improved from earlier versions we've tried.

The assembly quality is generally excellent, as you'd expect from Mercedes—a body that's solidly welded together, trim that fits, no rattles, nice (if not particularly lush) materials, good paint finish. All was not perfect, however, on this fairly early production example. The door handles and left seat adjuster were sticky, and the vacuum locking system wouldn't lock the right door. And though there was a total lack of any leaky wind noise around the windows when we began our test, some developed at the right front one 1000 miles or so later.

This test was longer than our usual one. We picked up the SLC in New Jersey, drove it into New York City for a day and then to Wilton, Conn., from where we began our long trek across the U.S. through the southeastern states, Texas, New Mexico and Arizona to our home base in coastal California. This 3500-mile journey subjected the SLC to a tremendous variety of conditions, as the reader can well imagine. New York was its usual summer self, 90-plus degrees and jammed. Here the SLC's air conditioning kept us cool and the engine never got over 230°F—cool as a cucumber, relatively speaking.

A hard rainstorm in New Jersey brought out two things: the first-rate behavior of the Michelin XVR tires and the excellent windshield wipers. Later in the trip, we used the wipers ⟫→

65

in rain at speeds up to 90 mph and found them still adequate. We do wish, however, that they would park farther down; they look pretty ugly to the driver, sticking up there above the instrument panel top when they're parked.

Later on, during the final leg across the desert toward San Diego, we found that the SLC's air conditioning, supposedly identical to that of the SL which we found wanting last year, was fully up to the job of keeping us cool in 110°, sunny weather. There were no rear-seat passengers for comment on conditions there, but at least the front seat was quite comfortable at an A/C setting just short of the full-tilt position that shuts off outside air.

A few more criticisms on interior matters. The sunvisors have a bent outboard edge that allows them to fit snugly against the ceiling when out of use, but this same bend prevents them from being positioned fully down against the windshield. We'd suggest a floppy edge like that in the Chevrolet Camaro to solve this slight annoyance. The electric windows are snail-like getting up and down. And the attachment of the shoulder belt to the lapbelt buckle is poorly designed: a slip of the elbow, or a push in the wrong place when securing the belt to its center fixture, will undo that shoulder belt.

In engine-transmission performance the 4.5-liter Mercedes models are a long way from the high-revving, jerky-shifting 6-cylinder Mercedes that acquainted the younger members of the R&T staff with the marque. This relatively large-displacement engine, used in the SLC, SL and 280-300 sedans, is a quiet, smooth unit that teams with an also smooth 3-speed torque-converter automatic transmission to give the sort of performance Americans expect in a luxury car. The combination isn't exactly quick, taking almost 11 seconds to get up to 60 mph, but it is effortless and about as responsive as we have any right to expect in these days of emission-controlled engines. And the electronic fuel injection keeps 1972-style drivability problems to a minimum. Things are rather leisurely getting off from a standing start but once the engine gets above 3000 rpm it begins to feel quite strong and even has a nice, subdued sound of power as it approaches its 5800-rpm limit. Fuel consumption is heavy: the 15.5-mpg figure is for everyday urban-suburban driving with the air conditioning off, and in highway cruising at 80-90 mph with the A/C on we got 12.5-13 mpg. The tank, supposed to take 23.8 gallons, took a maximum of 19.5 even after driving miles with the reserve light on, limiting cruising range to little more than 200 miles at high speed. The low fuel economy is a penalty we're all going to pay for emission control and low-octane fuel: the European version of this same engine, with a 9.0:1 cr and more advanced spark timing, would do 2 mpg better under the same conditions.

Mercedes' 3-speed automatic, new last year and used only with the 4.5 V-8 so far, is outstanding. Under most conditions its upshifts and downshifts are quite smooth, although a part-throttle upshift at low speeds can be a little rough. But its most laudable trait is its instant response to anything the driver wants from it. If he accelerates briskly in 2nd gear, then suddenly eases up, the gearbox doesn't hang about; it upshifts. If he selects a gear manually, he'd better be serious about it, for the gearbox shifts right then. And although drivers not used to it say it takes some acclimatization, the smoothly gated lever on the central console lends itself to manipulation without diversion of the driver's attention.

What about the chassis—ride, handling and braking? "Exemplary" describes all three. The SLC shares its chassis with the SL, of course, and this is Mercedes' most up-to-date engineering. The ride is about as good as it can be with steel springs and still be firm enough to give the kind of handling a Mercedes must have, and this holds true for any kind of road surface. As we've said of other Mercedes, the ride gets more impressive as the road gets worse. Drivers find they don't have to slow down for bumps and dips any more in a car like the SLC. We judged its ride somewhat better than the SL's.

The handling starts with M-B's ever-great power steering, quick (only three turns lock-to-lock) and, except for the low effort, as realistic in feel as the best rack-and-pinion manual steering. From there one can trace it through sophisticated suspension geometry that gives near-neutral response across the whole range and allows a slight, easily controllable oversteer to be induced by a burst of power or a quickly lifted throttle foot—a delight to the experienced driver but no threat to the inexperienced one. Finally, delivering all this to the ground were those great XVR tires on this test car—so good that they gave the SLC a quarter-g more cornering power than the lighter SL did on Dunlop SPs. One caution on these tires: for all their marvelous behavior one pays a price. They are wildly expensive to replace (well over $100 per tire) and they do not give long tread life.

Braking? Look at the figures. The stopping distances from 60 and 80 mph are both outstandingly short, and the average driver won't have any trouble keeping it under control while stopping like this though the rear wheels do want to lock up. We were surprised to get a little fade in our regular fade test, but it isn't enough to quibble about.

The newest member of our staff had a succinct way of summing up the 350SLC: he said that it is "the most complete car" he had ever driven. What he meant was that everything was done thoroughly. Everything hangs together; no loose ends anywhere. It's next to impossible to find fault with the car.

Controversy aside, nobody on the staff thought the SLC a beautiful car. That's subjective. But evaluating the engineering is an objective matter, and there's no question that it's the best. This car does its job well—from ambling around town to high-speed cruising to flailing about a winding mountain road to keeping its occupants comfortable and serene through it all. For $15,000 one expects a lot—and in the SLC one gets it. ⬛

COMPARISON DATA			
	Mercedes-Benz 350 SLC	Jensen Interceptor	Citroen SM
List price	$15,000	$14,500	$11,805
Curb weight, lb	3820	3905	3270
0-60 mph, sec	10.9	7.4	9.3
Standing ¼ mi, sec	18.4	16.0	17.4
Stopping distance from 80 mph, ft	253	300	300
Brake fade, 6 stops from 60 mph, %	12	25	nil
Cornering capability, g	0.725	0.750	0.722
Interior noise @ 70 mph, dBA	71	n.t.	n.t.
Fuel economy, mpg	15.5	12.0	15.9

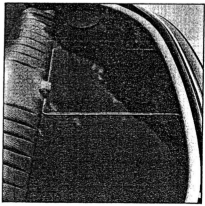

Lift-up lid on package tray reveals first-aid kit.

R&T ROAD TEST

MERCEDES-BENZ 350SLC

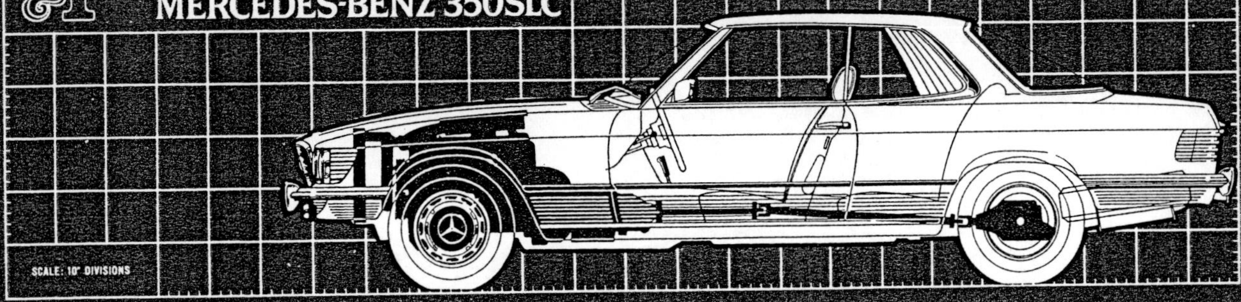
SCALE: 10" DIVISIONS

PRICE

List price, east coast....est $15,000
Price as tested,
east coast ....est $15,000
Price as tested includes standard equipment (air conditioning, automatic transmission, power steering & brakes, stereo AM/FM radio, fog lights, etc). dealer prep

IMPORTER

Mercedes-Benz of North America
158 Linwood Plaza, Fort Lee, N.J.

ENGINE

Type .... sohc V-8
Bore x stroke, mm ......92.0 x 85.0
Equivalent in............3.62 x 3.35
Displacement, cc/cu in......4520/276
Compression ratio 8.0:1
Bhp @ rpm, net........195 @ 4500
Equivalent mph.................... 109
Torque @ rpm, lb-ft......259 @ 3000
Equivalent mph...................... 72
Fuel injection........ Bosch electronic
Fuel requirement......regular, 91-oct
Emissions, gram/mile:
Hydrocarbons......................... 1.80
Carbon Monoxide 18.8
Nitrogen Oxides 2.04

CHASSIS & BODY

Layout ....front engine/rear drive
Body/frame .... unit steel
Brake system.......... 10.9-in. vented disc front, 11.0-in solid disc rear; vacuum assisted
Swept area, sq in................ 451
Wheels ....steel disc, 14 x 6½ J
Tires........ Michelin X 205/70VR-14
Steering type............. recirculating ball, power assisted
Overall ratio 15.6:1
Turns, lock-to-lock.................. 3.0
Turning circle, ft................. 37.9
Front suspension: unequal-length A-arms, coil springs, tube shocks, anti-roll bar
Rear suspension: semi-trailing arms, coil springs, tube shocks, anti-roll bar

INSTRUMENTATION

Instruments: 160-mph speedometer, 7000-rpm tach, 99,999 odometer, 999.9 trip odo, oil pressure, coolant temperature, fuel level, clock
Warning lights: brake-on, alternator, fuel level, hazard, high beam, directionals, seatbelts

DRIVE TRAIN

Transmission ...... automatic, torque converter with 3-sp planetary gearbox
Gear ratios: 3rd (1.00)........ 3.07:1
2nd (1.46)........................ 4.49:1
1st (2.31)........................... 7.10:1
1st (2.31 x 2.50) 17.7:1
Final drive ratio.................... 3.07:1

CALCULATED DATA

Lb/bhp (test weight) 17.8
Mph/1000 rpm (3rd gear)......24.0
Engine revs/mi (60 mph)...... 2500
Piston travel, ft/mi................ 1400
R&T steering index 1.14
Brake swept area, sq in/ton......221

MAINTENANCE

Service intervals, mi:
Oil change.......................... 4500
Filter change....................... 4500
Chassis lube .... none
Tuneup 9000
Warranty, mo/mi............12/12,000

GENERAL

Curb weight, lb 3820
Test weight 4085
Weight distribution (with driver), front/rear, %.................... 55/45
Wheelbase, in 111.0
Track, front/rear 57.2/56.7
Length 186.6
Width 70.5
Height 52.4
Ground clearance.......................5.4
Overhang, front/rear 32.7/42.9
Usable trunk space, cu ft........12.6
Fuel capacity, U.S. gal (see text) 23.8

ACCOMMODATION

Seating capacity, persons 4
Seat width, front/rear....2x21.5/49.0
Head room, front/rear......40.0/35.5
Seat back adjustment, degrees......60

RELIABILITY

From R&T Owner Surveys the average number of trouble areas for all models surveyed is 11. As owners of earlier-model Mercedes-Benz reported 3 trouble areas, we expect the reliability of the 350 SLC to be much better than average.

ROAD TEST RESULTS

ACCELERATION

Time to distance, sec:
0-100 ft.................................4.0
0-500...................................10.7
0-1320 ft (¼ mi) 18.4
Speed at end of ¼-mi, mph.... 80.5
Time to speed, sec:
0-30 mph 4.5
0-40 mph 6.3
0-50 mph 8.4
0-60 mph 10.9
0-70 mph 14.1
0-80 mph 18.0
0-100 mph 30.8

SPEEDS IN GEARS

3rd gear (5100 rpm) 124
2nd (5800) 98
1st (5800)................................ 62

INTERIOR NOISE

All noise readings in dBA:
Idle in neutral............................ 53
Maximum, 1st gear..................... 75
Constant 30 mph 64
50 mph 66
70 mph 71
90 mph 76

BRAKES

Minimum stopping distances, ft:
From 60 mph 125
From 80 mph 253
Control in panic stop ....good
Pedal effort for 0.5g stop, lb 17
Fade: percent increase in pedal effort to maintain 0.5g deceleration in 6 stops from 60 mph 12
Parking: hold 30% grade? ....yes
Overall brake rating ...... very good

HANDLING

Speed on 100-ft radius, mph....33.0
Lateral acceleration, g 0.725

FUEL ECONOMY

Normal driving, mpg...............15.5
Cruising range, mi.............see text

SPEEDOMETER ERROR

30 mph indicated is actually..27.0
50 mph 47.0
60 mph 57.0
70 mph 68.0
80 mph 78.0
Odometer, 10.0 mi 10.3

ACCELERATION

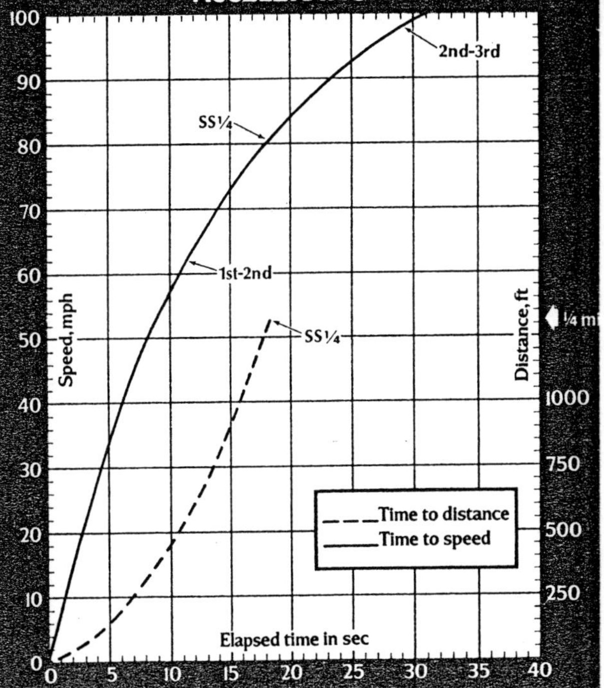
100
90
80
70
60
50
40
30
20
10
0
2nd-3rd
SS¼
1st-2nd
SS¼
Speed, mph
Distance, ft
¼ mi
1000
750
500
250
Time to distance
Time to speed
Elapsed time in sec
0
5
10
15
20
25
30
35
40

FIAT 130

THE AMERICAN MARKET may be retreating to smaller cars after a long period of overdoing it, but the Europeans are still working their way up the automotive ladder. In particular, business has been awfully good for Mercedes-Benz the last few years, Europe's prosperity supporting a healthy market for such medium-to-upperclass sedans, and BMW's 6-cyl models—if not as commercially successful as the Mercedes so far—obviously have a good future. So Fiat, Europe's biggest carmaker, wanted to get into this big-car game.

The car appeared in 1969 and it was called the Fiat 130. It was a 4-door sedan of the same general shape as a Mercedes 280—in fact the central body shell looked as if it were interchangeable—and between the 250 and 280 in overall size. It had a newly developed V-6 engine of 2866 cc and 140 bhp, independent suspension and disc brakes all around. It should have been competitive, except for one thing: its styling. It looked (and still looks) like an overgrown Fiat 124 sedan. And when a man, European or otherwise, buys an expensive sedan he usually wants it to look expensive, or at least handsome. Well, the 130 never made it, which must be a very sad story for Fiat not only because they poured lots of money into it but because the designers and

Fiat top management really agonized over its design. In 1970 the 130 got its engine tweaked from 140 to 160 bhp, and this year it becomes the 130-3200, indicating that its engine has been bored out from 2866 to 3235 cc, its power increased only slightly to 165 bhp (DIN) and its torque increased more substantially. Just as important, its interior has been completely revised—especially the instrument panel which has gone from a drab affair with band speedometer to a nice set of round instruments.

Far more interesting is the new coupe derivative of the 130, introduced at the same time as the revised sedan. It's built on the same "platform" as the sedan with 107-in. wheelbase, has the same mechanicals attached to the platform and even has the same instrument panel. But Fiat commissioned Pininfarina to lay over it a handsome new body, and PF has complied in a manner that gives me new respect for the time-honored body firm.

There's nothing startling about the coupe except its sheer elegance. It's a big car of conventional proportions with no styling gimmicks unless you consider clever sculpturing a gimmick. Let the photographs speak for themselves; my only criticisms of its appearance concern the gaudy wheels the extra-wide halogen headlights, and the U.S. version will undoubtedly have four round lights, taking up less lateral space and leaving more for the grille. Interestingly, the coupe (as well as the sedan) already meets current U.S. safety

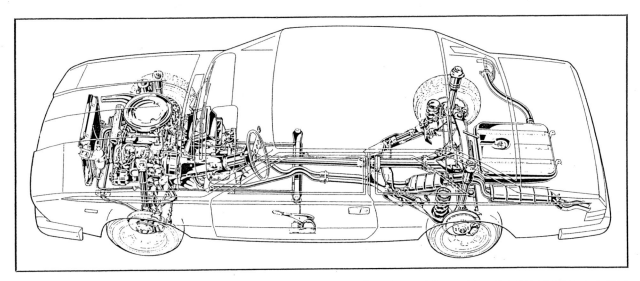

standards; they were taken into account in the basic design.

The engine is of Fiat design, not to be confused with the 2.4-liter, 4-cam, Ferrari-designed V-6 used in the Fiat and Ferrari Dinos. It has a cast iron cylinder block, aluminum heads, two overhead cams driven by a single toothed belt, inline valves and—especially in 3.2-liter form—extremely oversquare bore and stroke dimensions. Front mounted, it drives rearward through a standard Borg-Warner 35 automatic transmission and a 4.10:1 final drive. Ratios for this and the *optional* 5-speed manual ZF gearbox are given in the specifications.

Front suspension is of true MacPherson-strut type in that the lower lateral control arms depend upon the anti-roll bar for longitudinal certainty. But instead of the coil springs that usually go with MacP struts, Fiat has used longitudinal torsion bars like Porsche, anchored to a crossmember under the front seats and rotated by the lower arms. At the rear there's an interesting, unusual and seemingly complex set of linkages for the independent suspension. Large semi-trailing arms carry the coil springs and an anti-roll bar works between these without being attached to the body. The wheel hub carriers, not rigidly attached to the semi-trailing arms, are fixed to vertical struts (which include the shock absorbers), and

laterally located by the axle halfshafts themselves. Finally there are a pair of slim tie rods run from the carriers' rear sides to the crossmember on which the differential is mounted. Fiat has this arrangement patented and claims especially good wheel geometry and noise isolation for it; it is also significant that there are no splined halfshafts. But there may be some track change with wheel movement.

Brakes are vented discs with floating calipers all around, outboard of course, and assisted by a vacuum servo; there is a proportioning valve for the rear brakes which, via a simple linkage to the rear suspension as on the 124s, varies front/rear proportioning according to load and car attitude.

When in Italy recently I had the opportunity to drive a 130 sedan from Torino to Portofino and return in a coupe. Mechanically they are the same except that the coupe has slightly firmer suspension settings; the sedan had the standard automatic box and the coupe the optional ZF 5-speed.

The coupe is longer than the sedan and somehow, perhaps because of the firmer suspension, it seems much heavier even though the difference is only about 50 lb. Power steering (ZF) is standard in either case and with the new wide-section Pirelli steel-belted radials, it feels accurate and responsive; and there is plenty of cornering power from these tires. I ⟫→

The 130 sedan in its latest form . . .

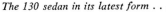

. . . and the coupe derived from it.

worked hard to keep up a good speed on the twisting, tunnel-and-bridge *autostrada* that took me most of the way and even when cornering hard at speeds over 70 mph the handling of either car was firm and reassuring. No problems here, nor with the brakes which several times were called upon to spare an overly bold Fiat 600 here and there.

V-6 engines are intriguing. They're not inherently well

FIAT 130 COUPE SPECIFICATIONS

ENGINE

Type	sohc V-6
Bore x stroke, mm	102.0 x 66.0
Displacement, cc/cu in	3235/197
Compression ratio	9.0:1
Bhp @ rpm, DIN	165 @ 5600
Torque @ rpm, lb-ft	
DIN	184 @ 3450
Carburetion: one Weber 45DFC (2V)	
Fuel required	premium
Emission control	engine mods

DRIVE TRAIN

Transmission	3-speed automatic or 5-speed manual
Gear ratios: automatic—	
3rd (1.00)	4.10:1
2nd (1.47)	6.03:1
1st (2.40)	9.82:1
1st (2.40 x 2.0)	19.64:1
5-speed—	
5th (0.874)	3.58:1
4th (1.00)	4.10:1
3rd (1.39)	5.71:1
2nd (2.08)	8.52:1
1st (3.87)	15.87:1

CHASSIS & BODY

Body/frame	unit steel
Brake type	vented disc; 10.8-in. front, 10.3-in. rear; vacuum assisted
Wheels	cast alloy, 14 x 6½
Tires	ER70-VR 14
Steering	worm & roller, power assisted
Front suspension: MacPherson struts with integral tube shocks; lower lateral arms, torsion bars, anti-roll bar	
Rear suspension: semi-trailing arms, vertical struts with integral tube shocks, and axle halfshafts for wheel geometry; lateral links to control toe-in; coil springs and anti-roll bar	

GENERAL

Curb weight, lb	3400
Wheelbase, in	107.0
Track, front/rear	57.8/57.8
Overall length	190.5
Width	69.2
Height	53.2
Fuel tank capacity, U.S. gal	21.1

balanced and the engineering has to be topnotch to get best results from them. Fiat has done such a job with this one; there's little to choose between it and, say, a BMW 3-liter for smoothness and quietness although it doesn't have the power of the BMW. And it has considerably more weight to pull around in this coupe than the BMW six does in the 3000-lb CS. But I reached the claimed top speed (slightly over 120 mph) easily in the coupe and have no reason to doubt the factory claim of 0-60 mph in 12 sec. This kind of performance, however, isn't going to make it very popular with the Stoplight Set.

A comment on transmissions: the automatic is better.

There's enough torque to handle it and it responds fairly well to demands for manual control. The ZF 5-speed is not worth the bother, being stiff and overly notchy as well as having a skewed 4-5 path that makes it very easy to wind up back in 3rd when you want to shift from 4th to 5th. Fiat plans to replace this with its own 5-speed later.

Fiat plans to market the coupe in the U.S. It may be a bit of a task to get Americans to pay the $9000 or so it'll cost for a Fiat, what with the make's "economy car" image in the U.S., but the elegance, size, automatic transmission and air conditioning should give it some kind of a head start over here. ◎

GÜNTHER MOLTER PHOTO

GEOFFREY GODDARD PHOTO

The 350SLC (top) is the 350SL with 14.5 in. spliced in between door and rear wheels, providing space for two more seats. Front and rear overhangs are unchanged.

H OT ON THE heels of the 350SL comes another new one from Stuttgart, the 350SLC. The 350SLC is the long-anticipated successor to the 280SE coupe, which was discontinued several months ago after a 9-year production run; apparently there will be no convertible to replace the 280SE coupe's companion model.

As the photos clearly show, the new SLC is directly derived from the 350SL, which is a new twist for the Mercedes model lineup. The SL wheelbase was stretched 14.2 in., new sheet metal was spliced into the middle to make a full 4-seater, and the SLC has an entirely different, fixed top. Front and rear overhangs are the same, all front-end sheet metal, the doors, windshield, lights and so forth are the same, so there should be some production economies not heretofore realized in the production of SLs, coupes and convertibles. The SLC is also 1.8 in. taller than the SL; but in comparison to its 280SE predecessor it's 6.5 in. shorter, 3.0 in. lower and 2.2 in. narrower. Track dimensions, shared with the smaller Mercedes 220-250 sedans, are also decreased from the 280SE.

The SLC is Mercedes' first big car to forsake the traditional grille form for the "sports" front end, and we wonder if this heralds the same thing for upcoming 450-series sedans. As regular readers will have noted, our reactions to the SL's styling have been cool and we had hoped the stretch job might work out better. We haven't seen the SLC in the metal yet—just these photos—but if they are accurate the stretch job is only moderately successful. The ultra-short rear deck, the long top and the louvered affairs in the rear top quarters (which appear to try to avoid an overlong side window) conspire to give the car a derived, overstretched appearance. But let's wait and see the real car before doing a styling critique. [*Ed. note: since this was written we have seen the car and these impressions were confirmed.*]

Mechanically the SLC is 350SL through and through. For Europe and other markets the engine is 3.5 liters, 200 bhp DIN, with a choice of 4-speed manual or automatic transmissions. For the U.S. it'll be the 195-bhp, 4.5-liter unit with 3-speed automatic only. It has the same unequal-arm front suspension, semi-trailing-arm rear suspension, vented disc brakes front and solid discs rear, the same fuel capacity but

a larger trunk, the same 205/70-VR 14 high-speed radial tires on 6.5-in. rims, standard power steering and so forth. Weight is up only 110 lb over the SL, so its weight is more reasonable relative to its size and carrying capacity and not much heavier than its predecessor.

The SLC should be available in the U.S. next summer, and if the interchangeability means any real economies, it might cost no more than the $13,000+ price the 280SE coupe brought before its discontinuance and the recent international monetary realignments.

MERCEDES-BENZ 350SLC SPECIFICATIONS

ENGINE

Type	sohc V-8
Bore x stroke, mm	92.0 x 85.0
Displacement, cc/cu in.	4520/276
Bhp @ rpm, DIN	195 @ 4500
Torque @ rpm, lb-ft	
DIN	270 @ 3200
Fuel injection	Bosch electronic
Type fuel required	regular
Emission control	fuel injection, engine mods

DRIVE TRAIN

Transmission...3-speed automatic (torque converter with planetary gearbox)

Gear ratios:

3rd (1.00)	3.23:1
2nd (1.46)	4.71:1
1st (2.31)	7.45:1
1st (2.31 x 1.96)	14.62:1

CHASSIS & BODY

Body/frame	unit steel
Brake type	10.8-in. vented disc front, 11.0-in. solid disc rear; vacuum assisted
Wheels	steel disc or forged alloy, 14 x 6½
Tires	205/70-VR 14
Steering	recirculating ball, power assisted
Front suspension:	unequal-length A-arms, coil springs, tube shocks, anti-roll bar
Rear suspension:	semi-trailing arms, coil springs, tube shocks, anti-roll bar

GENERAL

Curb weight, lb	3515
Wheelbase, in.	111.0
Track, front/rear	57.2/56.7
Overall length	186.6
Width	70.5
Height	51.2
Fuel tank capacity, U.S. gal	23.8

Mercedes-Benz

W107 Series 380SL

Specifications

Engine(s):   116·960
                              and 116·962

Number of Cylinders: 8

Cylinder arrangement: V-shaped 90°

Bore & Stroke: 88mm by 78·9mm

Displacement: 3839cc

Compression ratio: 8·3 to 1

Firing order: 1-5-4-8-6-3-7-2

Crankshaft bearings: 5

Valve arrangement: Overhead/hydraulic lifters

Camshaft arrangement: OHC, one per cylinder bank

Mercedes-Benz

W107 Series 450SL

Specifications

Engine: 117·982

Number of Cylinders: 8

Cylinder arrangement: V-shaped 90°

Bore & Stroke: 92mm by 85mm

Displacement: 4520cc

Compression ratio: 8:1

Firing order: 1-5-4-8-6-3-7-2

Crankshaft bearings: 5

Valve arrangement: Overhead/hydraulic tappets
                                   From 1976 with
                                   Continuous Injections System (CIS)

Camshaft arrangement: OHC, one per cylinder bank

Mercedes-Benz

W107 Series 560SL

Specifications

Engine: 117·967

Number of Cylinders: 8

Cylinder arrangement: V-shaped 90°

Bore & Stroke: 96·50mm by 94·80mm

Displacement: 5547cc

Compression ratio: 96·50 to 1

Firing order: 1-5-4-8-6-3-7-2

Crankshaft bearings: 5

Valve arrangement: Overhead/hydraulic lifters

Camshaft arrangement: OHC, one per cylinder bank

Mercedes-Benz

W107 Series SL and SLC

Model	Years of production	Chassis	Engine
Mercedes-Benz 450SL	1972 to 1975	107·044	117·982
Mercedes-Benz 450SL	1976 to 1980	107·044	117·985
Mercedes-Benz 450SLC	1973 to 1975	107·024	117·982
Mercedes-Benz 450SLC	1976 to 1980	107·024	117·985
Mercedes-Benz 380SL	1981 to 1981	107·045	116·960
Mercedes-Benz 380SL	1982 to 1985	107·045	116·962
Mercedes-Benz 380SLC	1981 to 1981	107·025	117·960
Mercedes-Benz 300SL	1987 to 1989	107·041	103·982
Mercedes-Benz 560SL	1986 to 1989	107·048	117·967

MERCEDES-BENZ 350SL 4.5

a driver's demand for downshifting, decidedly takes the edge off 350SL performance, leaving it—believe it or not—substantially slower in acceleration than the 280SL we tested three years ago. The very tall overall gearing (a 3.07:1 final drive gives 23.1 mph per 1000 rpm) has something to do with this too; it allows a high top speed—124 mph—but doesn't favor acceleration. At any rate, the 3.5-liter, 4-speed-automatic 280SE Coupe we tested last year, which weighed almost exactly the same as this 350SL, was much quicker and just as fast though naturally not so quiet and smooth.

The 4.5/3-speed combination also uses more fuel—10%, by Mercedes' own admission—though its use of regular fuel can offset that. It is thirsty: on a cross-country, fairly high-speed (70-100 mph) trip we averaged only 12.8 mpg using air conditioning, and the owner will do well to get our test mileage of 15.2 mpg.

It's in the chassis department that the 350SL has the clearest advantage over its predecessor. At the front, angled A-arms provide a moderate degree of anti-drive effect and get rid of the 280SL's severe front-end squash on braking. More importantly, the rear swing axles are gone, replaced by semi-trailing arms which keep rear wheel camber close to ideal in cornering. As a result the 350SL is thoroughly up-to-date in handling. Its much larger tires—70-series radials on 6½-in. rims—have more weight to cope with but still improve the SL's cornering capability from 0.674g (280SL) to an even 0.700g. That's with Dunlop SPs, which squeal a lot and are rather soft; perhaps the alternate Michelin XVRs would do even better.

The standard power steering, always outstanding, has been further improved and is slightly quicker than before. Its road feel is perfect, for a very simple reason: pull at the steering-wheel rim is absolutely proportional to effort required at the tires up to the parking-effort level.

Handling is close to neutral, a discreet amount of understeer being present under nearly all conditions to stabilize things. The tail will still come out if the throttle foot is lifted in a hard turn, but it does so gently and controllably and causes no problems. Perhaps the best thing we could say about the SL's handling is that we have absolutely no complaint.

The ride has been improved too. In the old car it was already outstanding, but the new SL is even better at taking monstrous bumps and dips than the old one. No matter what the road surface, you just keep on driving fast and the chassis (not to mention the absolutely stiff, rattle-free body) takes care of you. Amazing. And it's also utterly smooth on good roads too; very little harshness, pitching at a minimum, and so forth. There is no better combination of ride and handling.

Braking is very good too. No Mercedes has exhibited fade in our fade test for years, and the 350SL's ventilated front discs ensure that tradition is continued. The front wheels lock if you keep your foot jammed on in a panic stop, but there is no tendency for the car to get sideways and the driver will never be panicked by the SL's behavior in an emergency. For everyday driving, the vacuum boost seems to have been tamed somewhat from the 280SL, the pedal no longer being too light for gentle brake applications. Mercedes' anti-skid braking system will be available shortly after you read this; at this point it hasn't been decided whether to make it standard or optional. When it is available the SL will have the best passenger-car brakes in the world.

In summary, the 350SL is the ultimate in a 2-seat luxury car. Its great weight, luxury equipment and mandatory automatic transmission keep it from being a sports car or an entertainment machine, but if one desires merely to drive fast in supreme comfort and avoid the clumsiness of a big sedan, there is no better choice than the 350SL. 🐂

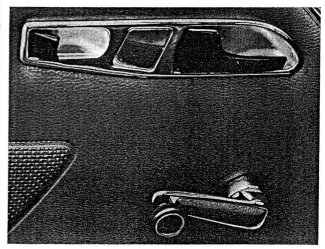